Out of the Ashes!

Ryan Anderson
Cohen
Errington

Out of the Ashes!

An Abuser's Story
of
Hope and Restoration

Carl Bishop

Books Bound to Witness
A Division of Rainbow's End Company
354 Golden Grove Road
Baden, PA 15005

Published by Books Bound to Witness
a division of Rainbow's End Company
354 Golden Grove Road
Baden, PA 15005

ISBN: 1-880451018-2

Library of Congress Catalog Card Number: 96-68496

"Behold, I will do a new thing; now it shall spring forth; shall ye not know it?"

Isaiah 43:19

Dedication

To my Lord and Savior, my wife and children, and my brothers and sisters in Christ!

CONTENTS

	Preface	9
1	The Early Years	11
2	The Imitation	17
3	The Beginning of the End	25
4	The Flight	29
5	The Other Victims	33
6	The Starting Point	37
7	The Old Man Died	41
8	Free toWitness	45
9	Lessons For Growth	49
10	A Matter of Forgiveness	53
11	The Power of the Holy Spirit	61
12	Overcoming Temptation	65
13	The Parole Board	69
14	The Window Cleaner	73
15	Work Camp	77
16	The Tests	81
17	The New Place	85
18	The Soft Steps	91
19	The Visit	99
20	The Examinations	105
21	The Prodigal Son	113
22	The Mind is the First Battlefield	117
23	Founded in the Rock	123
24	Work Release	133
25	The Perfect Job	141
26	A Church Famlily	149
27	Paroled at Last	153
28	Accountability and His Promise	161
29	The Invisible Line	169
30	Definitive Proof	175

31	Communication	179
32	A Vision Realized and a Vision Lost	185
33	Merry-Go-Round of Bureaucracy	189
34	A Promise Fulfilled	197
35	The Marriage	205
36	By His Grace	217
37	The False Accusations	221
	Post Script	229

PREFACE

As the author of this book, I want to preface my story with some declarations. The crimes and abuses that I committed were my own fault and I take full responsibility for these actions. No childhood traumas, no alcoholic binges, and no drug-induced stupors can be used as an excuse for my behavior. Though these circumstances contributed to the reasons behind my horrible choices, they can never be used as excuses for my selfish and destructive behavior. It was my decision to sexually use my stepchildren without any regard for their feelings or needs.

I also want to declare that, ***by the blood of Jesus Christ,*** I am forgiven for my *sins*. That's right, sins—not sociopathic, antisocial or addictive behaviors—but sins. This entire book is written from the point of view of one who is residing in the forgiveness and revelation of Jesus Christ.

As I relate my experiences, I will attempt to do so in the light of the knowledge that I have gained by the grace of His Spirit in renewing my mind and my thought processes. My personal belief is that Satan has intended to dismantle this nation with the systematic destruction of the family unit. One-sided families, dysfunctional relationships, gender confusion, and drug-and-alcohol altered families all serve to erode the foundation that has made this country a force in the world. If parents manage to escape Satan's grasp, the children are his next target. May this book be a weapon against the enemy and further the Kingdom of God!

Due to my sins, many were wounded. I allowed myself to be used by the enemy as a tool to destroy my own family from within. Today, I pray that, in Christ Jesus, I can now be used as a vessel and an instrument of healing and restoration, not only in my own family, but also in the lives of others who have been abused or committed abuse. As stated in Isaiah 58:12, I desire to be a rebuilder "*. . . the repairer of the breach and the restorer of the streets.*"

The express purpose of sharing my testimony is to reach both the abused and the abusers. If you are perpetrating sexual or physical abuse, you must stop now! You, as well as those who have been abused, can find respite from the terror and a place of healing in the loving arms of the Lord Jesus Christ.

Whatever successes I relate, whatever steps of recovery are revealed, and whatever miracles are described reflect the power of Jesus and are written to glorify Him. They are not of my own doing. It is also important to emphasize, in the strongest terms, the need for abusers who have experienced God's healing, to follow up with counseling, testing, and whatever requirements are necessary to determine that the healing is complete. I do not doubt the power of God to heal; however, I am only too aware of the persistence of the flesh to fail. Since we are new creatures in Christ Jesus, there should not be any hesitancy for that ***newness*** to be documented. The results will serve to glorify Jesus and to protect the community.

Chapter 1

The Early Years

Abuse is a generational sin. I found this to be true, not only in my life, but also in the lives of so many others I have come to know. The sins of my father were passed on to his children and I, for a time, ***was*** passing them on to my children. Through the love and forgiveness of Jesus Christ, this generational sin has been broken. My family now has a new heritage from God the Father.

When I was about thirteen, there was a time when I came close to *really* knowing Jesus Christ. Thanks to a kind neighbor, I had been attending the services at St. Peter's church on a regular basis. I could feel a Presence that I didn't understand but the feeling inside me was good. It was right. Then entered Satan who robbed me of that closeness—the hunger that we all have for the Lord. Once I turned my back on that Presence, the path to my downfall began.

Hungry for approval and acceptance, I would hang out with people who used me. I especially wanted to be wanted by girls and was convinced by Satan's schemes and lies that physical contact was equal to love. Because I equated this physical love with genuine acceptance and affection, I became willing to go to any lengths to get it. *After all,* I told myself, *this is how I prove my self-worth and value as a person.*

It was in my teens that I first became involved with pornography. I would fill my mind with the images, and then picture myself with various women, having their "love." It was addictive and my "habit" led me to buying coarser and coarser magazines. I didn't understand then how the enemy had begun perverting the healthy, pure and loving desires that God had created within me. Now, I realize that the sexual union of a man and woman in marriage is a wonderful gift to be enjoyed openly by two people who have made a lifetime commitment to one another. It is a spiritual relationship as well as a physical one.

Multiple partners! Satan whispered to me. *One woman will never satisfy you! You need multiple partners!*

Mainstream America was listening to the message of "free sex," and it was a message I was ready to hear. In my late teens, I began to see members of the opposite sex as objects created for my personal enjoyment—female bodies to fulfill my lusts and fantasies. There are spirits sent forth by Satan to oppress and direct us into this type of thinking and, with the advertising media as the primary perpetrator of such lies, many persons are deceived. In any area of beauty that the Lord provides, there will be counterfeits to confuse those who aren't strong in the Lord. This was me and, soon, what moral constraints I had were wiped away. Satan's lies and my own desires fed one another.

By eighteen I began to add to the oppression in my life by taking drugs and consuming alcohol. Opening these doors is the easiest way to add demonic activity to your life. In the Bible the words for "witchcraft" and "drugs" are the same. When you use them, you invite all the demons attached to them into your life. For me the drug progression was rapid and severe. At first I began by taking LSD and smoking grass. Then, after a few months, I tried shooting up morphine and, from there, went to shooting up speed or amphetamines. This continued for about a year until someone turned me onto heroin. Convinced by Satan that life was worthless, I resigned myself to dying. In fact, I had already tried suicide. . .

It happened just before I began using heroin. Spiritually blind and without hope, I bought the lies of the enemy. Two days after Thanksgiving, I played Russian roulette with a "twenty-two" automatic pistol. To help the odds, I had five loaded chambers and one empty one. I lost on the first try. Only a miracle saved me! I know now that the miracle was from a God who loved me and wanted me to know I had worth. But, when I recovered, I figured it had just been luck.

Instead of taking this wonderful new lease on life and doing something positive with it, I began using the heroin. This brought about many dangerous and life-threatening experiences, including the selling of drugs. The result was a prison sentence of twenty years with a minimum term of forty-two months. It was at this time when the enemy began to make the deepest inroads into my life.

As a pleasure seeker; alcohol, drugs, and physical contact had consumed my life. In prison I was surrounded by men and women who had spent their adult lives in seeking personal pleasure at the expense of their victims—people who were robbed of personal possessions, dignity, security, etc. In most cases the perpetrator's family are also his/her victims and are left to pick up the pieces of a shattered life, perhaps continuing a cycle of dysfunction. Many prisoners are often victims of a dysfunctional family unit. Generational sin comes into play as parents, uncles, and grandparents lead these young men and women into the prison system. Or, perhaps, the home environment encourages antisocial behavior and other personality problems.

Satan really feels like he has the victory in these prison situations. The hopeless are surrounded by the shattered. I know he gloats in all the human misery that abounds in these dark houses. Relationships are one of the true blessings of being in the family of Jesus Christ. Scripture is laced with wonderful promises in family settings and even gives those who are alone a new family. When we accept Jesus Christ, we need never feel alone again. We have a Heavenly Father who loves us and takes care of our needs.

In prison, the offender's family often disowns him/her. Most have never been properly skilled in establishing or maintaining relationships that are healthy. All of us know how to manipulate. Because human value is not recognized or acknowledged by many prisoners, there is the proliferation and acceleration of poor relationship skills. As loneliness triggered my debilitating life-style, I began to fantasize about being with women. My mind relived previous sexual encounters, reminding me of how much I was missing. Of course, it wasn't just me—the spirit of lust was rampant throughout the prison, causing some to turn to masturbation, homosexuality, and/or pornography. Others allowed the lust to fester, while counting the days to their release when they could act upon their desires. For me it was pornography—my addictive substitute for a relationship; however, I also wanted actual physical contact with women and lived for the day I would be released. Blinded by desire, I couldn't see the trap I was setting for myself. More and more this spirit engulfed me until I began to hate the very thing I wanted. The women in the pictures taunted me and I found myself seething with anger. Lower and lower I placed them in my value system as far as having any worth. Through pornography they teased me, whispering, "You can't ever have me—I'm out of your reach." Hatred seethed in me as I placed these "playthings" in the lowest of categories. Yes, I said "things"—things I wanted to possess and then throw away. I knew nothing about the preciousness of womankind as created by Jesus Christ and convinced myself that females were on this earth simply for the pleasure of men.

Oh, the blindness that comes when self is the god of our lives. How far we stray from the ideal of Ephesians 5, where the Lord, as the husband to the church, gives his life for her. In my mind, the reverse was true. *Women should service me, pamper me, and satisfy all of my whims,* I thought.. So blind, so blind . . . the spiral continued. As the time of my release grew closer, I decided I was not going to ever be in prison again. *This is no life for me,* I thought. *There's a lot I can do without being behind bars again. I just have to be smarter.*

To make a good impression, I put women on the back burner, and began acting "rehabilitated." I joined service clubs, spoke at high schools, and obeyed all the rules, barely recognizing the clean and sober me. Surprisingly, I discovered it felt good. Part of me wanted to keep this feeling, but, of course, Satan didn't like the change.

Chapter 2

The Imitation

The realm of evil I was about to enter was something I could never have imagined. Scripture tells us that when an unclean spirit leaves a person, the void must be filled with the Lord Jesus Christ. Otherwise, the spirit will return with seven other spirits more wicked than the first (Matthew 12:43-45). Although I didn't hit bottom immediately, I know that this is what happened to me. Satan, realizing I was blind to Jesus, was very patient; however, when the right time came, he struck.

After being released from prison, I enrolled in college and, by working all night and attending classes all day, I had my degree in three and one-half years. During college I met many women and stumbled blindly through the relationships, not realizing the value and worth that is inherent in each of us. Driven by my inward desire to "please me," I couldn't understand why the relationships didn't last. At first I refused to admit I was hurting the women but, as I began to sense my own loss of self-control, this slowly changed. But, still, I didn't stop—I couldn't! Although, I had a better handle on relating to women, I only used such sensitivity as another avenue for sexual contact. There seemed to be a battle going on in my mind between the "new man of the seventies" and the old man who was lost in self-gratification. The new man was real and caring—someone who wanted to be sensitive to the needs of others—especially women. He wanted to show love to others, to really care about them. However, the old man, who still lusted for pleasure and power over others, would not allow me to truly experience that new part of my personality. I became a good imitation of the new man, fooling most of my acquaintances.

At this point I met Rhonda, a woman who, as a child, had been sexually abused by her father and grandfather. This repeated abuse made her emotionally unstable and our relationship difficult because she would have drastic mood swings. One night she would be very affectionate and the next she would attack me with accusations.

"You don't care anything about me. You're like all the other men in my life."

"No, I'm not. Quit confusing me with your father and grandfather. That was then and this is now. We're both adults." I was incensed at the idea that she could have been used by her father in that way but, at the same time, I felt strangely excited at the thought of child-to-adult contact. Satan had planted the seed, introducing my mind to the unthinkable—a new kind of experience. The old forms of satisfaction had started to become boring.

"All you want from me is my body," she said accusingly. "You want to use me for a time and then throw me away."

"If that's true, why have we lasted so long?" I'd reply. But, inwardly, I knew she was right. More daring and forbidden actions had become necessary to achieve the excitement I needed. And so, I began to use violence as an expression of my emotions. I threatened her, hit her, and became a terror to her children. Everything between us would appear normal when something would set me off and I would become enraged, totally out of control. Both this woman and I were messed up emotionally and it was our very weaknesses that drew us to one another and kept us together for two years. It was a sick relationship, and, when she moved out of state, I never saw her again.

Today, after discovering my identity in Christ, I pray that the Lord will pour out His mercy on this woman and her children. It is important to understand that, as in her case, the effects of child abuse do not stop when the actual abuse or molestation ends. The confusion, hurt, anger and deep wounds go on and on. I met other adult women who had been abused and they, too, were dysfunctional in their relationships. When the enemy has control of your life, the destruction is passed on from perpetrator to victim and duplicated over and over again in all the lives that are touched by both of them.

Not long after this, I met Susan, the woman who would become my wife. When we first saw each other at the restaurant where she worked, the sexual chemistry between us was thick and explosive. She was pretty—and also nice. After a few dates, I knew that she was different and that I wanted to keep her as a permanent part of my life. The fact that she had two small children didn't deter me.

"I'm nearly through college," I said. "Let's talk about our future."

"Our future," she repeated. "I'm not sure what that means."

"It means I love you. It took a long time for me to find someone like you—someone I can care about. We're meant for one another."

She smiled. "My friends say we're a match made in heaven."

"Mine, too. And they're right. You're so sweet . . . so lovely." My voice was trembly. "And your children—Rebecca and Tommy, I would be good for them."

"You're very convincing," she said, her eyes sparkling.

"You've brought something special to my life—and my children seem to like you."

"Well then—?"

"I love you, too, Carl. And I need you!"

And so we started our life together in the flesh. Looking past the physical attraction, I think we were both fulfilling a need that had been lacking in other relationships. *If only we could have known the harm that our relationship would bring to her children. No, it wasn't a match made in Heaven. Just the opposite*. Through my allegiance to Satan, our lives were going to be hell. I say allegiance here to emphasize that either you are a son of Jesus Christ or you are a servant of Satan. There is no middle ground.

I had begun to drink about six months before we met. Nothing too heavy, just cocktails now and then and an occasional party drink. But it was enough—enough to open the door for the spirit of alcoholism to come into my life. Having been an addictive person before, I should have seen the trap; instead, I played into Satan's plans. The unhealthy lusts, now smoldering within, would soon be rampant under the influence of alcohol.

"Carl, I love you," she would say over and over again. "You fulfill my needs—*all* of them."

"And you are everything I could want—smart, aggressive, sexy, beautiful. You make me feel so special. The physical part has never been better."

"Me, too," she would say. "We're great together."

I knew Susan was being truthful. Never had I been so appreciated, desired, and in constant demand. I really felt that someone finally loved me. *Oh, if only I could have given as much in return—could have stayed satisfied.* But, without Jesus Christ in one's life, there is a constant search for greater and greater fulfillment. There is a search for that person, activity, or experience that will fill the strange hunger—the something that is missing within oneself. You keep looking for it in the world, but it isn't there. Only Jesus Christ can make you whole. Romans 8:20 tells us that the Lord gave us an emptiness so that we would seek after Him. The desires I had were all being vented toward people and things that could never satisfy me. Only Jesus gives this existence meaning, purpose, and fulfillment.

After dating for a few months, we thought it was time to be together, so she moved in with me. Then we married and, just before finding a house, we got possession of Susan's children. This started a lengthy court battle for custody between us and her ex-husband. However, he lost and from then on the children were with us. She had a four-year-old daughter and a five-year-old son. Rebecca and Tommy were the kind of children that dreams are made of—beautiful, warm, loving, sensitive, playful, innocent and so well-mannered. And then when Susan and I had a child together—Jennie—I had everything any man could want. All of my life I had looked forward to being a father—one who was more a part of my children's lives than my own father had been. Yes, I wanted to be the kind of father who played, laughed, and cried with his kids, showing that he cared. *Isn't it just like the enemy to pervert the most cherished of our thoughts?* But, I can't place all the blame on Satan because, once again, there were choices I could have made that would have kept me from sexually abusing the children.

One of the worst decisions we made was in the area of bathing. Susan and I thought that it would be all right for us to shower with the children to save time and to make sure they were washing properly. It seemed like a normal thing to do but, in reality, it was a horrible decision. As my stepdaughter began to grow, I starting looking upon her in a sexual way. The showers got longer and my "help" in washing her became more involved. Before long I began to involve my stepson in these abuses which grew progressively worse. It is not important that I go into the details of the assaults, but I want you to be aware that these children suffered repeatedly during that lengthy period. Their lives became a living hell; they never knew when that door would open and the horror and fear would begin again. Wound after wound I inflicted upon their minds and bodies. Their spirits were being crushed by the hand of the man who was supposed to be their protector. The man who was supposed to love them and keep them safe had become the nightmare of their lives. To further add to the pain, I began to drink very heavily. Because the shame and guilt of my actions could not be faced in a sober mirror, I numbed myself with alcohol; however, never did I take any steps to stop the assaults. Although shame was my constant companion and guilt was my shadow, I never displayed a willingness to stop hurting these children.

Along with the drinking came more violence. The children would never know which person was coming home—the man who was nice to them on the surface or this vicious person who would slap them and beat them for little or no provocation. *The fruition of the seven spirits was far worse than the demon of addiction that had already been in charge of my life.* The demons had been given an assignment: "Use Carl to make these children hopelessly angry with God." Of course, not only the children would be affected, but also their mother and all others who learned of the abuse. Satan's plan was working perfectly since I had become the willing instrument of sorrow.

As the assaults moved from weeks apart to days apart, and with my drug usage now at fever pitch, I began to feel that any female, in or out of my house, was fair game for my desires. Adultery, child abuse, pornography, alcoholism, drug addiction, hatred, bitterness and unhappiness was my life-style. Another drunk, another drug high! It was endless and hopeless.

But for all the confusion that was going on in my mind, I can't even imagine the thoughts that Rebecca and Tommy were going through. They must have asked, *What kind of a God would allow this man to continually hurt us? What kind of world is this? Why doesn't someone help us?* In reading about a woman who had been abused as a child, her response, when asked if her father had hurt her, was, "No, he only violated the innermost part of my being."

And I was doing the same thing to my stepchildren! They were constantly being violated and betrayed by someone they had once trusted. *What would be the results of these assaults on their lives in two, five, ten, or fifteen years?* Only the mercy and healing of the Lord Jesus Christ could ever help them. They were being taught by me that they were only useful as an object of someone else's desires and that to love was to surrender their bodies. To them being loved meant being sexual —being hurt. They would ultimately be covered with a victim spirit—a smothering cover that shuts off light to the soul. Satan uses such assaults and abuses for exactly these purposes. These children would grow up to be targets for every wicked and foul spirit which recognized their past wounds. In essence I had given them a spiritual and emotional death sentence.

The controlling spirit of the abuser uses fear, threats, and outright violence to keep everything secret. If no one knows what is being experienced by the children, he tells himself that the children will not know just how abnormal and perverted the assaults are. The children may sense something is wrong, but this person, who is supposed to love and protect them, keeps assuring them that touching them is all right. The perpetrator has to maintain secrecy because, if his or her actions were brought to light, the sanctions of the normal social order would come into play. If the perverted actions are not spoken, the victimizer begins to justify his or her actions.

By using alcohol and drugs, I could keep the secret. Sure, I knew how terribly wrong I was, but the overwhelming desire to satisfy my lust superseded all concern and moral resistance. I was driven, even battling physically with myself, to leave them alone, but I would not turn to anyone for help. All my sorrow and remorse were only coverups to assuage guilt and allow me to continue to satisfy my own deviant desires. Only my own needs and desires were important.

Please hear the cry of one who has done so much damage and begin to let Jesus Christ touch the core of your soul so that you will be free of the guilt, shame, and unrelentless hurting. Only Jesus can free you from the bondage that has held you in this terrible spiral—this downward whirlpool that has drawn you further and further into perversion. Stop wounding others. This hour—this very minute—confess your sins to Jesus Christ and allow Him to do a work within you that will bring a stop to the sorrow, hurt, and pain that your actions have caused, not only to children and families, but also to yourself. God cares about ***all.***

Chapter 3

The Beginning of the End

One February afternoon I came home from work to find my wife weeping alone in our home. Playing my role as the loving husband, I rushed to her side. "Susan, what's wrong?"

As she looked up at me through tear-filled eyes, I saw a hurt that I shudder to remember. "How could you? How could you?" she asked.

"How could I what?" I asked, pretending ignorance. I felt weak inside—sick to my stomach. *She knows*, I thought. *She knows what I've done!*

She stared intensely at me—as though trying to reach into my mind and pull out the truth. "The school nurse called." She paused, struggling for words. "Rebecca—she wanted to talk about Rebecca."

I tried to make my voice normal. "Is she sick? Has she been in an accident?" My acting was good—after all I had been role-playing most of my life.

"Rebecca went to the school nurse; she told her things—terrible things that you've done to her."

Every part of me wanted to run from that room and hide forever; every possible lie and defense rushed to my mind. Instinctively, I searched my wife's face for a sign of weakness, or perhaps even pity, but there was none. She looked devastated but also determined. There was a hardness about her which frightened me.

What can I do? What can I say? I asked myself. Finally, the words came out, "Yes, I have been molesting Rebecca." With this admission, an unbelievable weight was lifted off of my shoulders. That terrible oppressive, secretive guilt was gone. Today, I can truly say, "Thank God for that school nurse. Thank You for placing someone there for my stepdaughter." From the moment Rebecca had talked with her, it had become a safer world for her and other potential victims. On my own I had not been man enough to stop my injurious and destructive acts.

Having been exposed, there was no more hiding or running away from the consequences of my actions. Now, through the course of legal requirements, I would be forced to confront and deal with the corrupt concepts I had in regard to the rights of other human beings.

For the next nine months, I was involved in evaluations and counseling to specifically deal with my deviant behavior. As I began to understand the depths of the wounds I had been inflicting upon my victims, *some* remorse began to creep into my thinking. Not terrible remorse or sorrow, but just enough to make those around me think I was really sorry. The truth is that, even though I did not want to hurt my stepchildren any longer, there was no true repentance or grief. My selfishness had not changed.

Part of my rehabilitation was intended to help me stop drinking, but it didn't work. I couldn't stop. And, even though the spirit of deviance had been revealed, it was not gone. Nor could I break away from all the other spirits that had a hold on me. On my own, I was powerless. I rationalized that from now on I would only be involved with willing victims. Satan was totally brainwashing me. Every demon that I had previously invited in through pornography, alcohol, drugs and immorality raged within me. I was literally out of control. Me, me,me was all I could think of. Confused, without a clear thought, my downward spiral continued, taking me to the depths of despair.

One night, six months earlier, I had wept because of my destructive behavior. My excesses were abounding and yet, in spite of my tears, I made the choice to keep right on hurting my stepchildren. Inwardly, I had started to search for spirituality, but God seemed so very far away.

Now my mind ran nonstop as I did everything I could to get out of this mess and back on a *normal* path—at least what I knew to be normal. Drinking twenty-four hours a day provided an escape—a relief—but this soon subsided. While undergoing treatment in a program for sexual offenders, I did not live at home. Child Protective Services had required that I move out of our home so that the children could remain there with their mother. This arrangement worked for a short time but, one night, when I went to pick up my wife, she was not there. Convincing myself that I needed to check on the children was easy to do. Besides I missed them! Again I was concerned with *me* and not the fact that this was the number one violation of my treatment program. Being in the house with a victim without supervision would not be tolerated no matter what the circumstances.

Within two weeks, I was thrown out of the program and recommended to be sent to prison as a danger to society. And it was true. I was a danger to others—especially children.

The judge who sentenced me to prison made only one mistake: he gave me a week to set my affairs in order. After this I was to report in on my own. Fat chance!

Chapter 4

The Flight

What followed was a last-ditch effort to control and terrorize my family. Because of my prior outbursts of anger and, of course, my demented condition, the family was afraid to say no to any of my plans. To their utter amazement, I told them we were going to move to another state and begin life all over again.

Susan tried to reason with me. "Carl, I don't think this is a good idea. They'll find us. And besides, how will we live? We'll need money!" She agonized over her every word.

"We have to go, or I'll be in jail. Don't you even care? Quit being so selfish and think of me. And what about the kids that everyone is so worried about. How will you ever provide for them?" Once again I imposed my desires on them —taking advantage of their victim mentality.

"But how will we live?" she asked again. "We have to eat!"

"We'll sell the furniture and everything we don't need. After all, we're starting over; we'll buy new things."

It was a dream short-lived. In twelve days, fifteen hundred miles from home, I was apprehended while my family was left stranded without money or hope. The police were tipped off that I was staying at my brother-in-law's home. Our family had been waiting to receive some money from the sale of a few possessions we had left behind.

When the telephone rang, I answered it expectantly.

The party on the line sounded formal. "This is Western Union. I'm calling in regard to a Mr. Carl Bishop. Is he going to be there to receive the money which is being wired to him?"

Realizing that Western Union didn't have my telephone number, I ran for the door and into the waiting arms of four detectives. When they asked who I was, I finally made a decision that benefited someone else other than myself—my brother-in-law. This man, who had taken my family in without asking questions, had given me a touch of the Lord Jesus Christ. He had come to the Lord about a year before and didn't need to get into trouble for sheltering a known felon. A calm came over me as I turned to them and said I was their man.

In a frenzy, I was handcuffed and whisked into the waiting police vehicle beyond the fence. When I came out of the gate, I was amazed to see eight or ten other police cars up and down the street. They were apprehending a vicious molester who had fled from another state. *I was that molester.*

Through the window I could see my wife staring at me, tears in her eyes. They were probably tears of relief. The children were still in the motor home, and did not see me taken away. I was thankful for that. In reality, it probably would have brought them a measure of satisfaction to see me being handcuffed and roughed up.

Numb and dazed, my wife went about the task of getting our few possessions and the children back to their home which was 1500 miles away. She, not just the children, was also one of my victims. My family would be living with limited finances, trying to cope with all the emotional turmoil that I inflicted on them. It wouldn't be easy but at least they had been rescued from further injury—thanks to the person who called the police on me. Because I was going to prison, they were being set free.

Society sends abusers to prison, often providing treatment programs and educational opportunities for them. This is well and good, but there must also be help made available to their victims—whether strangers or family members. These persons may be suffering from physical, financial, and emotional injuries. Also, whenever possible, the perpetrator should be required to financially compensate his/her victims.

Me—I had no problem when it came to getting back to my home state. I was being returned through the courtesy of the legal system. My wife and children came to see me before I was sent back. They were reserved but polite. My wife was numb; the anger had not yet set in.

"Are you doing okay?" I asked.

"My biggest concern is getting us home!"

"I'm sure the relatives will help."

"They've been—been good to us." She was near tears as she looked at the children. "They're enjoying the visit."

Today, I want to thank the person who called the police and told them of my location. It ended my reign of terror and gave my family a chance to breathe—a chance to heal. They had been slowly dying—not living. It's called "soul death."

Chapter Five

The Other Victims

Prison may be a terrible place for offenders but the people left behind are also prisoners through no fault of their own. My wife became a prisoner of her own self-blame and of society. Since she had allowed me to abuse the children, she felt responsible. Admittedly, there are times when the other parent has to accept some responsibility for the abuse in that they may have ignored unusual behavior or personality changes in their children. Also, if the spouse of the offender was abused as a child, he/she may not understand how to avoid the inevitable generational cycle. But the ultimate blame must be placed on the perpetrator. It was his or her choice to molest.

My wife was left to deal with limited finances, children who were suffering emotionally, and her own poor self-esteem. Her trust had been crushed. Over and over she asked herself, *How could I have loved someone who could do such a heinous crime?* She put up barriers to loving relationships — barriers which took much work to bring down.

When the non-offending spouse has trouble with the children, resentment and some aberrant thoughts and questions begin to creep in. *Did my child have any blame in this?* It sounds unbelievable, but after the wounds have been inflicted and the fabric of lives unraveled, Satan rushes to fill one's mind with such irrational thoughts.

The guilt and shame increase as society looks at the non-offending parent in terms of possible guilt. Over and over this "other victim" thinks, *If only I had—. What if I had—? Why didn't I—?* In truth, the perpetrator bears all the responsibility for his or her assaults. Though outsiders may want to cast blame on others, it is always the offender's crime. As members of the family try to pick up the pieces of their lives, they may need counseling—something the offender should pay for. The remaining parent sometimes has to bear the accusations of their own children who ask," Why didn't you protect us?" The accusation breaks the parent's heart since he/she is asking the same question of themselves. There seems to be no answers.

And what about the devastation to the children? *How will they be able to relate to other adults? Will their response to authority be permanently corrupted? What type of people will they seek out for relationships?* The victim spirit that has been introduced into their lives will manifest itself in various means so that victimizers will be aware of that weakness. The wounded person is not aware that they're sending out these signals. And so abused children often end up in abusive adult relationships. They have learned that to be loved is to be hurt. Part of the sphere of love is this terrible wounding they must endure.

Often, in sexual abuse, the very thing the victims hate is the activity they begin to be involved in. Promiscuity is often a result. The level of their self-esteem drops to zero. Since they feel so worthless and cheap, it does not matter what happens to them or who does whatever to them. In First Peter 1:18b, we are told that the ungodly father only passes on worthless and empty examples of behavior. In these cases, they are worse than empty—the behavior patterns are even abnormal for the secular world.

There is a need in every child to be confirmed and affirmed by his parents—especially the male parent. When this affirmation has been replaced by abuse, the ability of the child to relate to a loving Father God has also been damaged. *How can someone want to be loved by a Father God when his earthly father sexually or physically abused him?* Satan has a hand in this sorrow. He comes to kill, steal and destroy. The destruction of the family is one primary way he uses to destroy our nation. Human regard is continually lowered through abuse.

The children are left to grow up with mixed and dysfunctional behavior patterns. Loving may be out of the question. Being loved may never happen. The ability to accept the tender and outstretched hand of Jesus Christ may be difficult. But if this occurs, there is hope. What Jesus Christ can overcome in moments, could take many years of counseling to bring about!

Chapter 6

The Starting Point

"Except the Lord build the house, they labor in vain that build it." Psalm 127:1

Before there can be any hope applied to a situation of brokenness and destruction, Jesus Christ must be brought into the picture. It is my belief that the starting point for the offender is Jesus Christ. Confession must be made to God in the name of our Lord Jesus Christ. There must be acceptance of the Risen Savior into one's heart by faith, resulting in forgiveness and cleansing. Only after this step has been taken can any real progress be made in realizing the terrible harm that has been inflicted on so many. In the following pages, I will relate the many miracles that took place in my life and in that of my family after I took this most important step. I wish to state again that every miracle and all recovery for my family and myself is totally to the glory of the Lord Jesus Christ.

Within minutes after my arrest, we had entered the downtown area. The officer turned and asked a question that so many would later ask, "Why would you do that to a child?"

I had no answer. I was guilty and had no defense. As I looked around, I noticed that my car door was not locked. We were in the middle of a traffic jam. *Perhaps I could push open the door and run for it. Just maybe I could lose the officer in the crowd.* But the news I had heard only the night before kept me in the car. Arizona had passed the fleeing felon law that allowed the use of deadly force. If I ran, I would be shot down. *No, I would sit tight; my running was over.*

The day was warming up. Before long it would be over one hundred degrees. I was taken into the basement of the county jail and led to the counter where the booking officer asked me the question I had heard earlier, "How could you?" Again, I had no answer.

I was put into a cell which I estimated, judging from the number of bunks and the tendency of county jails to overcrowd, would hold about fifteen men. "You can expect lots of company before the day is over," the officer said. Then the metal cell door closed and made its all too familiar sound. The sound made it seem so final. A thousand emotions began to crowd my brain as I fought the intrusion of tears. Yes, the big, bad, child molester wanted to cry. There I was, feeling helpless, and staring at what could be twenty years in prison with no family, no future and no direction. I felt helpless. All of this misery and hopelessness had been brought on by my own sin—my selfishness. There were no excuses to offer. It is times like this that Satan wants to rush in and tell us that life is not worth living. *Do not believe him!* As long as we're alive we have hope! As long as there is a loving, merciful, forgiving God, there is life!.

Sitting down on one of the bunks, I tried to take a deep breath. All the effort of holding back tears was making it difficult for me to breathe normally. *Be tough*, I thought. *The other prisoners can't come in and find you crying*. But another part of me didn't really care. I just wanted to have all the misery and sorrow of my life over with. It would be better for my family—for me—for everyone.

It was at this moment, the lowest point of my life, that a

miracle began to unfold. All the words previously spoken to me by Christians began to come to my conscious memory. Even when I had not been receptive, there had been many people willing to share the love of Jesus Christ. This should encourage all of us to take *every* opportunity to tell others about Jesus. The words will not return void—they can bear fruit at a later date.

Oblivious to my surroundings, I knelt down on the cement floor, opened up my arms and asked the Lord Jesus Christ into my heart. "Lord, I am a sinner and—and I've made a terrible mess of my life. I know I need to be covered by the blood of Jesus—to have my sins washed away. I can't do anything to help the plight of my family, but You can! I need Your love, Your mercy, and Your strength to go on." The tears, now flowing in a heavy stream, created a pool of water on the cell floor.

Years of hurt, sorrow and fear were washed away in that stream! Yes, I knew without a doubt that the Lord Jesus Christ, according to His word, had forgiven me of my sins. Though I didn't hear Him speak audibly, the Spirit embraced me and His love became a shower over me (Romans 5:5-10). I was washed in the blood of the Lamb. *I mean literally washed in His blood.* To this day, I still remember and have reexperienced the sensation of His blood pouring down over me.

Many people are skeptical when it comes to jail-house conversions—and rightfully so. A desperate criminal will do anything to convince others that he/she has had a supernatural experience which changed them. Perhaps they want special prison privileges or to serve a shorter time because of good behavior. God alone can judge hearts but eventually the truth of their conversion will be known. He knew that I yearned for the spiritual—not something the world could give me.

Chapter 7

The Old Man Died!

It was November 7th when the old man died in that cell. When I came up off my knees, I belonged to the Lord Jesus Christ. By accepting His offer of His redemption, I became His purchased possession. *My life was never to be the same!* Looking back, it was as if the very glory of Jesus Christ had flooded my cell as He swept off the chains of Satan from my life. A window of heaven had been opened and I found my true heritage—the family of Jesus Christ. *My Father and my God, I love you.*

If there were a word that was greater than exhilaration, I would use it now. There is no way to express the total relief that was upon me. A loving God guided my steps; I was a man with a purpose. The cell was my dance floor; I could not stop smiling. Even my blood cells were smiling. Choirs of angels were voicing their joy that another person had been plucked from the flames. All of my life I had wanted to belong to something—to someone. Always searching for an identity, I never seemed to fit in. Now, at last, I belonged. Though undeserved, my God had rescued me from death. *Thank you Jesus! Thank you for caring so much!*

As I sat on my bunk, hope was rising up in my heart. Life was being breathed back into my veins. I was alive! My mind began to focus on the task that lay ahead. *How many years of prison must I serve? How could I become more intimate with the loving God I had just met? Basically, where did I go from here?* Being newborn into the faith, I didn't know how to go about walking in the kingdom of Jesus Christ. All I could do was cry out to Jesus—it was the only thing I knew how to do. It is a lesson I want to remember. No matter how long we have been in the faith, it is still by His power that we have our success and direction (Zechariah 4:6).

"Lord Jesus" I cried, "I know that you have changed me but I don't know where to go from here. Won't you please help me?"

Inwardly, I heard His reply. *Learn my Word.*

Of course, I thought, *I will read the Bible.*

It was Monday, however, and there would be no church services for a week. *How could I wait that long to start this new life with my Lord?*

Soon others began coming into the cell. First just a couple, then a few more, then others. It was getting very crowded. I was removed from that cell and put in the next one. It was smaller but there was no one else in with me. This made me happy. However, this soon changed as others joined me. Before the evening ended, this ten-man cell would hold over forty men. Amazingly, tempers were not flaring.

By 10:00 PM, I was moved again into a very large cell—one big enough for perhaps sixty men. By 1:00 PM there were 120 men in that cell. There was only room enough to stand. If you had to go to the bathroom, you gave up your spot next to the wall and would have to stand out in the open cell area. With temperatures in the "one hundreds," the smell was becoming nauseating. It wasn't until 10:00 AM that we were taken out for showers and assigned to the various cell and prison areas for confinement. I was taken to another county area that was used for short-term or out-of-state prisoners and, while waiting for my hearing, stayed there for about ten days.

After being assigned a room, I asked when the next Bible study would be available. Hearing that it would definitely not be until the following Sunday, I went to the phone to call my family. *Wouldn't they be happy that I had received the Lord Jesus into my life?* They were not. The reality of who I had been was still too painful for them to see me as anyone but the brutal man who had terrorized them. That really confused me at the time. I talked to Phil, my brother-in-law, who was just ecstatic at my conversion. When I asked him for a Bible, he said he would rush right down and bring me one. Later, I found out that he gave me his own Bible. What a willing sacrifice! He was so joyful to hear of my conversion that nothing was too great a sacrifice to ensure my growth. Phil and his family are still treasured brothers and sisters in the Lord for our family.

Within two hours I had Phil's Bible. I rushed into my new room and sat down on the bed, feeling very happy. This was all I needed. But, as I looked down at the Bible, I realized I didn't know where to begin. So much to read, but where? Again I could only call out to the Lord Jesus Christ, "Lord, where do I begin?"

I heard his voice, *Begin at the beginning.* And so opening the book to Genesis, I read, *"In the beginning God created the heaven and the earth."* How many times had I read or heard that? For the first time it had meaning. My God had created the heaven and the earth. And now this new beginning was mine. *"And the earth was without form and void...and the Spirit of the Lord moved upon the face of the waters."* (Genesis 1:1-2) The Spirit of the Lord was now moving on my life which had been without form or substance. How wonderful you are, Jesus! With a great hunger I continued to read the Word of God.

In the county jail cells, you have all day to spend on any activity you choose. From ten to fourteen hours per day, I read God's Word—stories I vaguely remembered hearing, movies of characters now so completely revealed. *Oh, how I love your Word, Lord. It brings instruction to the simple.* God's love for me and all of mankind was being revealed through the Old Testament. New beginnings, Noah and the flood, Moses, other characters, and examples of God's love filled the pages. It was so exciting! Oh, how I praised God for giving me such a hunger for His words.

After nine days, authorities came and told me that if the state where I was wanted did not show up the next day, I would be set free. All of a sudden, I began to think about escaping from this life-style my own way. Although I really loved God, I was still unlearned in the ways we must keep ourselves on His paths. By His grace, the state authorities arrived in the morning and I was flown back to my state.

After spending only one week in the county jail, I was to be transferred to prison to begin my sentence. During that week I'd continued in the Word. Something was going on inside of me but I was not sure what it was. Now I realize that it was the transforming of my mind through the pure words of the Lord. We were in four-man cells with six people. Though I tried to tell some of the others about this wonderful Jesus I had found, they didn't seem interested. And so most of the time, I just read and prayed.

The following Tuesday morning, they called my name for the prison bus. After being shackled hand and foot and chained with twelve other men, we were led to the vehicle. As we went out into the open air, we could see armed guards watching our every move. Because there had been past attempts to free prisoners during this time, they were taking established, normal precautions. One luxury had been afforded me—I had permission to carry my Bible onto the bus. As we traveled to prison, I read the Bible, excited that this captive had been set free.

Chapter 8

Free to Witness

The prison was all too familiar since I had been at the same facility only eleven years earlier. I knew that Satan would have me believe that I belonged in a place like this; however, he was and is a liar. Through the Lord Jesus Christ, all mankind was set free from worldly prisons. Although my body was physically incarcerated, I had been transformed by the renewing of my mind. Jesus had died for me!

I was put into a two-man cell and spent the next six weeks waiting for the Classification Committee to decide where to send me. Because I was now in my late thirties, I could go to any of the maximum security prisons. The weeks were spent in taking psychological tests, IQ tests, personality tests, and physicals. Even though all of us were assigned to counselors, we only saw them once or twice.

While we waited in the receiving center, we were kept in our cells for twenty-one hours each day, getting out for one hour of exercise and three meals. What a wonderful benefit —all that time to devote to the Word of God. Blinded to the truth for so long, I needed all the light I could get. I still do.

One thing was becoming very clear to me. My conversion had not resulted in a "better me." I was a new me. The miracle of salvation had created a new person who had a loving nature, a caring heart, compassion, mercy and a giving disposition. It wasn't the old me abstaining from my previous perverted behavior. Instead, there was the knowledge that the new me had never been involved with those sins. To be sure, Satan continually tried to fill my thoughts with perversion and ungodly thinking but I grew to recognize that these were not my thoughts. My thoughts had all been brought into captivity to Jesus Christ (II Corinthians 10:5). In reading Philippians 4:8, I learned that good, pure, holy, and virtuous things should be filling my thoughts.

Do you understand what I am saying? Carl Bishop is not a recovered child abuser. He is a *delivered* child abuser. Instead of holding on to the hope of never hurting children again, I press into Jesus Christ to reach a fullness in my service to Him. To be sure, there are still choices to be made after deliverance—choices that keep me from being entangled in the yoke of bondage. By His grace, I have made many good choices. One example was my decision to have two years of Christian Counseling with a Christian therapist when I was released from prison. The Lord knew that I needed to learn to identify my behavior and gain new insight as to the pain I caused my victims.

Although, there was no doubt in my mind that the blood of Jesus was and is enough to wash away all of my sins—enough to deliver me completely, I realized that all knowledge comes from God and that He uses wise counselors, pastors, doctors and others to help us fight the enemy. Also, I knew that God would be glorified by the counseling and treatment sessions. The miracle He did in me would become a witness to others. *After all,* I thought, *If the Lord's work is so wonderful and complete in me, then I should not be afraid to let others know about it—and to have the experts test it.* Scripture tells us that a candle is not hid under a bushel but is set out so that it gives light. It was and is my desire to display the glorious light of Jesus Christ—to tell of His marvelous work. By being obedient I would continue to grow spiritually.

But, for now, the proof of my convictions would have to wait—even though I had the inward assurance of deliverance. I was beginning what could be a ten-year prison sentence. *Lord, watch over me,* I prayed.

By this time, my Bible exploration had taken me to Psalms. I was in Psalm 91 when the Lord gave me my first personal promise from His word. Before I read this Psalm, I tried a certain tactic taught to me by one of the neighbors who had witnessed to me. She said that when we needed to hear from the Lord, we could just open the Bible and, after praying for guidance, wherever we put our finger on the page would be where He directed us. At the time I thought that was a wonderful idea. I opened the Bible to Numbers 35:21. The end of the verse reads, "*. . . the avenger of blood shall put the murderer to death when he meets him.*" I almost fell over. Here I was at a new point in my life, asking the Lord what He had in store for me during this prison stay. *Surely it wasn't death! This must be the wrong place,* I thought. *I'll try another place.* So I asked the Lord again what to expect in this wilderness trek. Opening the Bible, I came to Judges 21:5, and the end of that verse read, "*. . . who failed to assemble before the Lord at Mizpah should certainly be put to death.*" I began to sweat. *What are you saying, Lord?* Fear came over me. I wondered if the Lord were pronouncing the end of my earthly life. I shuddered. *Perhaps*, I thought, *if I try just one more time, I will find the true direction from the Lord.* Praying fervently, I begged for direction. With one eye open, I slowly opened the Bible. Perhaps if I moved a little further from the beginning of the Bible, I would find the true direction. I put my finger on a verse and looked down to II Chronicles 23:7, which ends with, "*. . . anyone who enters the temple must be put to death.*"

The Bible fell from my lap. Tears began to well up in my eyes. I was certain the Lord was telling me that I would be killed during my prison term. Because my sins had been so grievous, I would have to die. *But*, I thought, *God is just. And didn't I deserve death? Accept your punishment instead of feeling sorry for yourself.* Sinking to my knees, I held up my hands to the Lord, saying, "Lord Jesus, you are just and righteous in all of Your acts. I have sinned terribly and am worthy of death. I belong to You—may Your will be done. I thank You for forgiving me of my sins and I welcome the privilege of coming home to be with You now. I beg You to heal my family and erase the memory of my hurt. Oh, my Father, take me home." I closed my eyes and waited for the stroke to fall.

A few moments went by and nothing happened. I opened one eye and looked up. I was confused. *Had I heard correctly? Was death for me?* The Lord immediately took me into Psalm 91. *"I will say of the Lord, He is my refuge and my fortress; my God in him I will trust...and under his wings will you find refuge. You will not fear the terror of night, nor the arrow that flies by day...a thousand may fall at your side, ten thousand at your right hand, but it will not come near you. If you make the Most High your dwelling...then no harm will befall you...for he will command his angels concerning you to guard you in all your ways...because he loves me, says the Lord, I will rescue him."*

Now I understood. The old man had died but the new man was His property and He would be my shield and strong tower. Man should not cause me fear but I must learn to fear the Lord. He alone was to be my fear. *"If God is for me, who can be against me?"* (Romans 8:31) In the prison setting, showing weakness is dangerous. Everyone puts on a mask of toughness to protect themselves; however, God's promises assured me that I didn't need to fear other prisoners. This knowledge set me free to be his witness in the prison system.

Chapter 9

Lessons For Growth

Throughout this book, you will read about the wonderful changes Jesus has made in me. It is important for readers to understand that many of these experiences came about only after the Lord had repeatedly given me lessons for growth. Trusting Him, progressive sanctification, and sharing His wonderful love was a long process. The Lord gave me the perseverance to keep trying, and I had the presence of mind not to let go of His merciful hand.

One of my sins had been profanity. It seemed as though I rarely finished a sentence without including some swear word. Even after being delivered, I didn't press to remove this sin from my life. Although I seldom swore, any such words were a terrible witness of my new citizenship. It was easy to rationalize my behavior and tell myself that I was doing just fine. *After all*, I thought, *my language has improved eighty percent.*

After about two weeks in the prison, they put a man in my cell who swore ten times more than I ever had. No matter what we talked about, profanity and perversion spewed out of his mouth. By the end of every day, I felt polluted. The "words of garbage" seemed like a heavy weight, trying to pull me downward. Every foul word, every sexual reference, every insidious laugh brought inward pain to my spirit. Two weeks with this man seemed like two years. One night I cried out, "Lord, please transfer this man from my cell. The profanity is so disgusting."

The Lord answered me, *Your mouth sounds just like his to my ears.*

Talk about being convicted! Instantly, I realized how lazy I had been in attacking this area of sin in my life. "Please, Lord," I prayed, forgive my hardness to sin." This man spent four more weeks in my cell and, although I talked to him about the profanity, it never deterred him. It was, however, a constant reminder for me to watch the fruit of my mouth. And I do mean constant! As I was moved around to different prisons in the coming years, this man always ended up being sent to the same facility with me. I knew this had to be the Lord's doing and that He was also providing me an opportunity to plant seeds. "Thank you, Lord," I prayed, knowing He would water and cultivate them through other saints.

After a few more weeks I was sent into the main population. Because child abusers are normally targeted for attacks and abuse, I was somewhat concerned. It was time to put my trust in Jesus to the test. Knowledge of His love is exciting, but experiencing it is freeing. Over the next three years, the Lord did, indeed, keep my crime private.

When I moved into my cell, I found out that one of the prison toughs had just moved out. I breathed a sigh of relief. One of the privileges of being in a cell first is to get that bottom bunk. It was mine! There weren't many Christians in our building, so not much of my time was spent socializing. The first week I was alone in my cell but every Tuesday there was an influx of new inmates from the reception center.

The second week, sensing that someone was going to be placed in my cell, I asked God for another brother in the Lord to fellowship with. When I went to work, I left my Bible open on my desk and, upon returning, I found this wonderful brother praising God for answering his prayer for a Christian cellmate.

He and I became very good friends.

The first time I went to the chapel to meet with the other worshipers and the chaplain, I was very disappointed. After exchanging greetings with the chaplain, he questioned me. "How are you doing?"

"Just great!" I replied. "I continue to delight in God's grace."

His response was not inspiring. "You've been in prison too long; it's affected your thinking."

Bewildered, I quoted scripture to him. "Paul says, *'I am content in whatsoever state I am in* (Phil 3:13 . . .)' so why shouldn't I feel good?" He had no answer. This, however, soured me from attending the chapel services.

Realizing I needed fellowship, I sought out a Bible study and became involved. There I became acquainted with a volunteer named Ron who was overflowing with the love and forgiveness of the Lord Jesus Christ. Week after week, he would come up and give us insightful words, a caring hug, and a listening ear. This is what ministry is all about. Repeatedly, I have thanked God for showing me, early in my walk, what it means to serve. With God's direction and grace, I can only hope to minister with as much openness and caring as Ron.

Chapter 10

A Matter of Forgiveness

Desperately, I prayed to be accepted into the work release program—even a work camp would be great. For the first time, I genuinely missed my family. Now that Jesus Christ had made a change in me, I wanted them to see and acknowledge it. *If only I can rekindle all of the relationships that I've destroyed,* I thought. Oh, how I wanted my wife to love me again. How I wanted my children to be at ease with me again. *So new in Christ, yet still so selfish*! That was me.

Because of the distance, the visits from my family were very infrequent. Even when my wife did visit, I could tell that the distance between us was greater than the miles that separated us. However, I acknowledged that it was miraculous that any of my family wanted anything to do with me. My deliverance and recovery did not heal the wounds I had created. Only the grace of the Lord allowed me to have continuing contact with them. Because my side of the family helped them out around the house and also with money and food, Susan kept up some semblance of caring about "us." But, the reality was, if she hadn't needed the financial support, she would not have visited me or continued our marriage.

Slowly, I began to accept that all the changes in me might not make any difference to my family. I had abused and terrorized them for years. Their ability to forgive and accept me into their lives again would have to be on their terms. Pleading with God to reconcile my family to me, I promised everything in the world. *If only He would allow me to be the husband and father my family needed. Oh, how I wanted to love them properly. Oh, how I wanted to give them direction to grow in their relationship with the Lord. Would I ever get the chance?*

It was at this time I became committed to loving them no matter how they felt about me. *Isn't this how Jesus loves us?* He had often extended His loving arms to me, doing wonderful things, but I had not responded. Just as God's love for me was unconditional, my love for my family could not be based on their acceptance of me or on our restoration. Instead of putting any requirements or restrictions on my love for them, I could only do what the Lord had done for me—lay down my life for them. I chose not to pray that someone wonderful would come into their lives to help them because I wanted to be that someone. I couldn't walk away.

During this time, the Lord was continuing to work on the excess baggage I brought into the salvation experience. Anger was still a problem for me. It was very easy for me to lose control of my emotions and to speak rashly. This anger was rooted in hurt for the abuse I suffered as a child, hurt for the lack of a loving relationship from my father, and hurt from being unpopular except as a clown. The angry outbursts, cursing, and violence were my feeble attempts to express these hurts. However, no matter what the source or extent of these hurts, I never had a valid reason to wound others. There were other choices available to me. Attempts to explain the behavior of abusers may be made, but excuses for such behavior are not valid.

One day, when playing basketball in the gymnasium, it got

real physical under the basket while rebounding. Someone hit me from behind and I immediately reacted by swinging my elbow to hit back. We both spun around and squared off.

"What do you think you're doing, Carl?" the other inmate asked.

"I got hit and was getting you off my back," I said. Breathing heavy, we were both ready to go at each other.

Another inmate cautioned us. "Cool it. The guards in the balcony are watching." We agreed but left only after making threats to one another for that night.

"I'm going to take you out of here and give you early parole in a box," he said

"We'll see who survives, pal," I sneered through clenched teeth.

On the way back to the housing unit, I was walking with my roommate—my brother in the Lord. He walked along side of me and let me fume. Pumping myself up, I was ready to do all I could to hurt this guy. My only hope would be to get him down and hurt him quickly. As I was clenching my fists and gritting my teeth, the adrenaline made my heart race a hundred miles an hour.

Ken turned to me and said, "What would Jesus do in this situation?"

I stopped in my tracks. *What was I doing? Had I forgotten that I belonged to the Lord Jesus Christ? This type of behavior was not becoming to a child of the Most High. I was supposed to be spreading the gospel—the good news about Jesus and His love—not spreading hatred and violence.* I looked squarely at my friend. "Thanks Ken for asking the question. I needed a reminder."

"We all do at times! It's a question I ask myself every day."

Later, back in my cell, I knelt down and began to pray. "Lord Jesus, I have sinned again by causing a conflict and inflaming it. Please forgive me and help me to straighten out this mess."

The Lord spoke to me, *If you want to correct this situation, you must apologize to the other inmate.*

I immediately broke out into a cold sweat. *Apologize*, I thought. *Apologize to Ralph. How can I apologize? This is prison and you don't just apologize in prison. I could just see it. "Oh, excuse me for hitting you in the face with my elbow."*

"Oh, no problem, it was probably just an accident."

To apologize would be a sign of weakness that would label me as a coward. This really worried me because when the other prisoners think that you will not stand up for your rights, everyone tries to take advantage of you. I didn't want to be in such a situation.

"Lord, there must be some other way," I begged.

Inwardly, I heard His voice. *You know I promised to protect you and to smooth the rough places. Trust me!*

"Okay, but everything I know tells me this won't work. Regardless of the consequences, I will do as you ask because I love You."

The other inmate lived across the hall from me. The hour was up and, when the doors opened, I went across the hall into his room, catching him by surprise. He was still sitting down and in a vulnerable position. "Ralph, when I hit you it was in the heat of the game and all of the action. I was wrong and I ask you to forgive me."

His mouth dropped open and everyone in the room stood in silence as if they couldn't believe their ears. Ralph stammered, "It's—okay; I understand."

"I'm truly sorry," I said again before going back to the day room area. Any moment I expected the other men to come and ridicule me for backing down. I thought, *Ralph is going to get into my face now that he knows I'm not going to fight.* Nervously, I waited but nothing happened. Fifteen minutes went by, then thirty, and soon an hour had passed. Still nothing! I was stunned. At the next break I went to my room, got down on my knees, and thanked the Lord. "It was just like You said it would be, Father. No one thinks I'm a coward. In fact, I feel they've gained some respect for me because I had the courage to apologize. Thank you, Lord, for showing me that Your way is always the right way. It doesn't matter what the outward circumstances appear to be."

I wish I could say that I never again tried to defend myself or settle things inappropriately. However, this incident did give me a guiding post for walking the Christian path when anger rises up in me. Through the Lord and His Spirit, I have learned how to use self-control in the area of anger. *Usually* I can hold my tongue and let my spirit-man rule instead of my flesh-man. More than anything, I learned to communicate my feelings when I'm angry before they build up to the boiling point. By refusing to hold resentment or bitterness toward others, I keep my temper from taking over my emotions. Through this incident, and by His grace, temperance began emerging as a personality and character trait.

Forgiveness was the next revelation that the Lord gave me. As I continued through the Word of God, His forgiveness for my sins became so wonderfully evident. *I truly was crucified with Christ. My sins are all washed away by the blood of the Lamb, the perfect sacrifice.* The Lord impressed upon me how complete His forgiveness is. No amount of recovery and no restitution could ever cleanse my past sins. Through the blood of His Son, I am truly redeemed from the pit, demonic oppression, and the power of Satan. All ties to the old man are severed. Christ's cross became my cross. I made the choice to live my life through and for the Lord Jesus Christ.

At this point, I feel I need to clarify my position. My sins of child abuse were terrible and caused much damage. The lives of my stepson and stepdaughter have been altered forever. Even with recovery, they have had to deal with wounds and hurts that they did not and do not deserve. Again, I state that I am fully responsible for my selfish actions; however, the Word of God reveals to me that His sacrifice on the cross was the complete payment for my sins. To continue to carry guilt and blame around would be denying the sacrifice of Jesus. It would be like saying that the forgiveness for this kind of sin not only requires the blood of Jesus, but also heavy guilt and sorrow on my part. That is, in itself, sin. His grace is beyond my belief. I don't know how He could justify me for all my sins and yet I know He has. His Word assures me that if I am willing to be a partaker of His grace and mercy, I am forgiven. *My sins are removed from Him as far as the east is from the west and thrown into the sea of forgetfulness.* (Micah 7:19))

As I comprehended His forgiveness, the Lord showed me how necessary it is for me to forgive others who offend me. Even if I were in the right, I could not hold a grudge or refuse to forgive. When I could not forgive others, I struggled with anger. Bitterness and pain gnawed at me continually. But the Lord gave me a way to be free from such turmoil. Scripture plainly tells us that if we do not forgive others, we will not be forgiven. (Mark 11:26)

Every attempt a person makes to grow in their Christian walk is defeated by unforgiveness. He or she should honestly ask questions of themselves? *Is there someone who hurt or offended me? Did someone in the church step on my toes? Am I upset with my spouse?* Whatever the offense, real or imaginary, it has to be released through the blood of Jesus. Maybe those who offended you don't deserve forgiveness, perhaps they haven't even asked for it. Keep remembering that Christ paid for the forgiveness that we don't deserve!

The Lord says to " . . . *leave our gift at the altar if we have ought against our brother and to go and be reconciled." (Matthew* 5:24) It has been said that when there is a wrong between two Christians, they should meet each other on the way to apologize.

Those who have been deeply hurt or wounded by someone they love or trust, understandably, find forgiveness very difficult. Victims may carry wounds for years and will continue to do so until they forgive. The act of forgiving is critical, not only to the wholeness of the one who forgives, but also to aid in the spiritual restoration of the offender. *But the actions were so terrible,* whispers Satan. *The people who hurt you so badly don't deserve forgiveness. It's too difficult to forgive something so painful. It's impossible to forgive!*

Deciding to forgive is one of the most important choices you will ever make! It is often more for you than for the one who hurt you. Through the help of the Holy Ghost, all who have been terribly wounded and scarred can be set free! The healing comes from exposing the hurts and allowing the Lord to set you free. What is impossible for man is not impossible for the Lord.

I have known many adults who were abused as children and still carry the victim spirit! Relationships are impossible for them because they have not dealt with their hurt and pain in a positive way. Of course, there may not be an easy or quick route, but I know that Jesus can and will set you free. Children who are abused often have a warped concept of loving and caring relationships. They ask themselves this question; *How can I love a Father God when the only father I knew sexually abused me, continually beat me, or betrayed me by living in a perpetual state of drunkenness?* Such persons must see the true loving Father who weeps every time His children are hurt. They must see a loving Father who has given mankind free will instead of robot minds.

Again, I must emphasize that victims have to face their pain! Burying the incidents or denying how they have affected their lives, will not bring about healing or transformation. Scripture promises that everyone can be set free by the truth. Psalms 62:8 says, *"Trust in Him at all times you people; Pour out your heart before Him; God is a refuge for us."*

Don't allow Satan to rob you of God's gift of abundant life. Let the grudge go! Let the bitterness go! Let the victim mentality go! Hold onto Christ! There will be a day of judgment. It may not be in your time but the Lord will defend you.

Chapter 11

The Power of the Holy Spirit

The first few months I was kept in a place called Duck Hall which was for the new arrivals. Inmates stayed here until they understood the institution's rules and procedures. Then, as space allowed, we were moved to the permanent housing units. After a couple of months I was moved to another unit. The permanent units only had single cells which I believed were much better. Finally, there was some privacy—some time alone. Even though my roommate had been a fellow Christian, always having someone in the room was, at times, a bit tiresome. I'm sure he felt the same way.

My Bible reading had taken me to the Book of Acts which spoke of miracles, wonders, and signs brought about by the power of the Holy Spirit. Reading of these things was exhilarating. If I could only tap into such power to help me, I could minister to others, but also walk in a more pleasing and closer manner with my Lord. There were various Scripture references to speaking in tongues. In Acts 2:4 they spoke in tongues so that men from seventeen different nations understood the message of the gospel. There were three thousand souls saved in one day. In Acts 8:17 we see that there were some new disciples who received the Holy Spirit when Peter and John laid hands on them. Acts 10:46 says that when these new believers received the Holy Spirit, they began to speak in tongues and to magnify the Lord. In Acts 19:6 the disciples spoke and prophesied when they had the Holy Spirit fall on them. My curiosity was aroused. *What was this special touch of the Holy Spirit? What was this speaking in tongues?* Remarkably, I could not find answers in the Christians I knew. Ron, the Bible study leader, believed in tongues but had never spoken in them.

With no one to guide me, I turned to the Lord and asked for illumination. "Lord, what is this gift that I am reading about? What is it for?" After following up in I Cor. 12 and 14, I wanted this gift. If the Lord had something for me that could help equip me to better serve Him, to teach me the truth of the Bible, to give me spiritual discernment, then I wanted this gift. I began to pray nightly for this "baptism in the Holy Ghost."

"Jesus, if there is this wonderful gift, I am willing to receive it at your hand." One night, some strange words suddenly came out of my mouth. They sounded like "um . . . ba . . .ba." How excited I was, feeling the presence of the Lord all around me. *This must be the gift*, I thought. "Umbaba, Umbaba" I repeated over and over. All that week I just kept taking the time to repeat this language of heaven. Then I let Satan rob me of what the Lord had given.

"Umbaba" he said., "You made that up yourself. It is not a gift from God. You are just trying to make things happen. This isn't real."

I sinned by believing his lie. *I must have made it up*, I thought. *I wanted to have this gift so much, I must have invented the language. Language,* my thoughts echoed, *a couple of sounds—not even one real word.* I felt silly for having spoken this "language" all week.

How totally foolish I was for not believing the Lord Jesus Christ! It is so like Satan to sow doubt in our minds and hearts, making us question whether the gifts and promises of God are really true. I had to repent of this sin and go back to the point of accepting the gift the Lord had given me. Using the language again, I began to feel strengthened. And so I asked for more! "Lord, if this portion of your gift is good, will you please increase it in me?"

Immediately I felt His presence. Words began streaming out of my mouth, words I had never heard before. For the next ten minutes I don't think I even took a breath. A fullness of language was now mine. "Oh, thank you Lord," I repeated over and over again. From that moment on, as I used my new language to pray and to intercede, I began to see things happening much faster in my life. Scripture was easier for me to understand. Now I was more aware of my sins and I knew how to seek deliverance from them.

Unbelievably, some years later, before I was released from prison, I sinned again by doubting that the gift of tongues was real. For a year I stopped using my prayer language and, during this time, everything went very slowly. Paperwork that should have been processed in a few days took weeks. At every turn, it seemed I encountered resistance. I didn't put two and two together—my sin of failing to use God's gifts and the things that were going wrong. By His grace I came to my senses and, about a year before I was released, I began speaking in tongues again. And just as quickly as everything that concerned my release and the restoration had slowed down, it began to speed back up. I was warring again in the heavenlies, putting the Holy Spirit and His plans into effect. How wonderful it is to be in agreement with the Lord and His purposes.

This chapter of my testimony is written to encourage you to seek this gift of tongues from the Lord. Search the Scripture for His direction. Allow the Lord to equip you for battle, for glory, and for victory. So many times when words would not come, I could only groan in my spirit. When my mind failed me in seeking direction for prayer, this language always had the answer. I'm giving the glory to the Lord for this gift which was meant to help His children be better able to accomplish the works He has prepared for us.

The presence of the Holy Spirit is also to lead us into all truth. He will teach us about Jesus Christ. He will bring us discernment in dealing with the enemy. It is by His Spirit we triumph over the enemy. The Spirit moves upon us to bring sanctification and to develop us into the image of Jesus Christ. In II Cor 3:18 Scripture says we are " . . . *changed into His image from glory to glory, even as by the Spirit of the Lord.*" I found that the Holy Spirit was necessary in all areas of my life, not just tongues.

For a man who had been a drug addict, an alcoholic, and an abusive parent, I had much growing to do. I knew that when the Lord Jesus Christ came into my life, I was delivered from all of my sins, bondages, habits, and oppression. However, we do not always walk in that knowledge. Even as the Lord called Lazarus out of the tomb and told the people to remove the grave clothes that bound him, we also need to have others help us remove those things which bind us—things we brought into our salvation experience. (John 11:43-44)

I experienced instant deliverance from alcohol and cocaine. There were no physical symptoms; in fact, I did not even miss them. My new life was so satisfying that I didn't struggle with resistance. My desires had turned to things above and not to things of the earth. It has now been over eleven years since that wonderful night of deliverance and I have not taken another drink or sought out drugs. The keeping power of the Lord Jesus Christ is phenomenal. Some of the translations for "keep" are guarding, High Tower, Fortress. These are words of permanence and longevity. A guiding, loving hand is always there to help when we need it.

Chapter 12

Overcoming Temptation

An area of temptation that Satan tried to use against me was the lust I had previously indulged in. Whether it was my strong addiction to pornography or my lusting after women, he tried very hard to convince me that the past was still with me. Satan is a liar. The images that my mind could still remember were thrown up to me continually. Every foul picture, every degrading act, and every perverted scene that he relished, invaded my thoughts. Since I had the mind of Christ, I knew these were not truly my thoughts but an attack of the enemy.

I asked the Lord for help with this battle. Only if we entertain Satan's thoughts and images can they be a problem. In I Cor 10:13, Scripture says, "*There has no temptation taken you but such as is common to man: but God is faithful who will not suffer you to be tempted above that you are able; but will with the temptation make a way for you to escape, that you might be able to bear it.*" For me, the way to bear the temptation is to acknowledge right away that the thoughts are not my own. I refuse to dwell on any of the images or sexual thoughts that the enemy tries to put into my mind. At first this was a real struggle, but the more I fought and the more I was willing to obey God and cry to Him for strength, the easier it got.

Every time I said no to the enemy, I found new strength for the battle. One of the verses that was so helpful to me was II Cor 10:5 "C*asting down imaginations, and every high thing that exalts itself against the knowledge of God, and bringing into captivity every thought to the obedience of Christ.*" During my struggle with the enemy, the Lord gave me some very simple instructions: "Don't look upon any pornography, read provocative material, or dwell on ungodly thoughts."

At this point, I need to reemphasize how important the Holy Spirit is in fighting these battles. It is He who empowers us and points us to the Word for a sword to fight with. We cannot do it on our own strength. If we will humble ourselves enough to ask the Lord for help, we will be exalted in victory for His glory. In later years, I realized how great a lie my sexual fantasies were—how great a lie my urgency for sexual contact was. In surrendering my will to the obedience of the Lord's will and word, the joy, the fullness, and the utter delight that I received from normal relationships was astounding. Satan had deceived and robbed me of God's best.

Sexuality is an enjoyable and beautiful gift from God when experienced within marriage where there is loving and sharing, giving and taking, and a strong emotional and spiritual commitment between husband and wife. The sick and hurting relationships that I was once involved in cannot be compared to the tender, loving, joyful union that I now experience under the authority and blessing of the Lord in my marriage. I'm telling you that you have not known joy or fulfillment until you submit your sexual life to the Lord. We are all His, and every aspect of our life belongs to Him. This is no great revelation for most of us, but for me it was one of the utmost importance. Realizing that no area of my life could be separated from my relationship with Jesus was an important factor in my battle against temptation. A strong sex drive has been the downfall of many saints as Satan tries to pervert and steal a beautiful God-given gift. I plead that you not allow yourself to fall for his lies.

Jesus Christ gave me victory over my past. He showed me the way, gave me the power, and helped me through every temptation and battle. "Oh, Lord, I magnify your name. This chokehold of perversion has been utterly crushed by my obedience to your Word and through the power of your Spirit." Just as the Jews came into Canaan and the Lord drove out seven other nations before them, He was driving out the ungodly nations of my inheritance. These nations were the sins and abuses that had once held me in bondage. The Lord destroyed them on the day of my deliverance, and now He was showing me that *"He who the Son sets free is free indeed."* (John 8:36)

Chapter 13

The Parole Board

As the Lord continued His work in me, I was acutely aware of the nearness of my sentencing date by the Parole Board. In this particular state the judge sentences offenders to the maximum for their crime — five, ten, twenty years or longer. Then the Parole Board determines how much of that time will be served. In making their decision, the Board considers past offenses, the severity of the new crime, age, and the prosecutor's reports.

Counselors, who handled about fifteen cases each, would help us get our papers together and try to accommodate us when we wanted some type of action from the institution or Parole Board. My counselor called me in about a month before I was to appear before the Board. His words were not encouraging. "Since this is your third felony and, because of your age, you can expect the Parole Board to be very severe with your time. Child abuse is an heinous crime and the Board has been giving out very long sentences in cases such as yours."

"Wha — What are you saying?"

"That you should be prepared to receive a sentence from between seven and ten years."

I was speechless; however, my initial reaction was that I

deserved every minute of the ten years. Yes, the blood of Jesus Christ had washed away my sins, but I had caused so much pain and sorrow to others. My sentence was nothing compared to the long-term effects my victims would suffer because of my selfish and destructive behavior. If I served ten years, it would be much less than I deserved.

This acknowledgment sent me back to my cell, humbled and emotionally drained. The new hope that had been brimming in me seemed so distant now. *Seven to ten years*, I thought. *If I'm doing all that time, I can't repair the damage I've caused. I can't try to restore the emptiness. And Oh Lord, I want to do this so much—so very much!* I knelt beside my bed and cried out to God. "Father, I know that my sins are worthy of death and yet I only have to serve a few years. Thank You for showing me grace and mercy."

Yes, I was praising God in all things, determined to accept His will for my life; however, the desires of my heart would not be silenced. No longer could I continue the charade. "Oh, Lord," I cried, "my heart is set for the work it will take to restore my family. How can this happen if I don't see them for ten years?" My battle with the flesh continued as I went back and forth from God's will to my will. "Lord, I don't know how I will do all of this time but I do know that with your help and the empowering of the Holy Spirit I can make it. My life belongs to You. Your will must become my will and desire. Cleanse me of the need to tell You how to run my life and do with me as You will. I am Your servant." Though young in the Lord, I knew that I would never be satisfied unless I followed and accepted the circumstances that the Lord brought into my path.

Just because I had come to the Lord did not mean that I would not have to serve my full time in prison. Although the Lord sometimes dramatically curtails or even cancels some sentences, I do not know what the criteria is for such a move except that such cases are clearly for His glory. Again, I went to my knees. "Lord, I come before You and ask for a miracle. You know my sins and my background. I acknowledge that it is just that I face at least seven years in prison but I ask for Your mercy and intervention with the Parole Board. No more than three years Lord—let the Board give me no more than three years!" *Was I greedy? Was I still just self-seeking?* No! I believe that my motives were right—that my heart was right.

Preparing my family for the worst, I told them that it would be at least five and maybe eight years before I would be released. My wife, at the time, said she would wait; however, in my mind I begin to write my family off. My daughters would be nearly grown by then, and my son—he would be twenty-one. *Perhaps I should do them a favor and stay out of their lives.* Then God could bring them someone who would minister to them and provide the kind of love they didn't receive from me.

The Lord shook me out of the self-pity stupor I had put myself in and reminded me that I was a new creature. With the Son in me and with the power of His Spirit to help me, I would be the man they so desperately needed. I began to regain confidence. My faith began to climb. I did not know the time I would have to serve, but I did know that, through the Lord, I could be a Godly influence on my family. They were my children, given to me by God, and His power would ensure that they would be protected and even blessed because I was their father.

When the day came to see the Board I was ready. Because I had been praying and fasting during the week, I entered the room with a confidence that was unrelated to the circumstances. Regardless of how much time I did or didn't get, I belonged to the Lord and that was what really mattered.

The men whom I faced were considered two of the toughest Board members. The spokesman's face was very solemn. "After reviewing your case and the records that have been sent to us, we have decided to set your minimum term at three years. We will give you another review in about a year. Do you have any questions?"

Somehow I managed to say some appropriate words before I rushed back to my cell. "No, I don't have any questions. I look forward to seeing you then."

While praising Jesus and savoring this victory, a thought crossed my mind. I asked the Lord for no more than three years and I had received only three years. *Perhaps I should have asked for only two years.* That may sound strange but sometimes we limit the Lord by only believing for small miracles when He is capable of huge miracles. Today I ask for great miracles, knowing that I serve a marvelous, miracle-working God.

Chapter 14

The Window Cleaner

After receiving my sentence, I settled in for the long haul of three years. With good behavior, I would be allowed to go to a work camp in about eighteen months. From there I would go to a work release facility and then hopefully to parole. I had my plans all set without consulting the Lord.

During this time, I began to ask the Lord to help me cleanse myself from the memories of sin that had been so dominant in my life. I wanted to specifically remember and confess my every individual sin. No, I was not looking for a second forgiveness. When I accepted Christ into my life, my sins were permanently forgiven; however, I wanted a personal release from any hold the enemy might have over me. Satan throws our past up to us every opportunity he gets. Kneeling in my cell one evening, I asked the Lord's help in remembering my past, ugly sins so I could confess them, repent, and then move on. Again, this was not for assurance of forgiveness; however, acknowledging the depths of my depravity helped me understand the depths of His love and forgiveness.

During the next hour, many of my past sins were revealed to me and then taken to the foot of the cross and mentally left there. The abuse came first—each incident—each hurt—each vicious act. My unfaithfulness to my wife followed, then my failure as a father in regard to physical and mental abuse. As I put my sins, one by one, under the blood of Jesus, I began to feel this tremendous sense of relief. I was disarming Satan from using the past against me. The cleansing was now mine in a practical way that I could understand. I would encourage you to follow this example of cleansing so that you can stand against Satan when he taunts you with his accusations. He asks, "Is there a sin you have forgotten? What about the time when—?" On and on he goes with his accusations, trying to steal peace of mind. By keeping us in the past, there is no time for us to develop the character of Christ.

Dealing with my sins individually was very freeing and empowering. By naming the animals, Adam exercised his power of authority over them and, by naming my sins, I felt the freeing power of Jesus Christ within me. When Satan reminded me of some past sin, I would recall how I had taken that to the cross and left it there. And if he actually came up with a sin I had not repented of, I stopped right where I was to repent of that sin.

With this new sense of freedom, I began to delve into the Bible once again. Reading it completely through the first time was a breath of fresh air. Even to this day, when I read His Word, I feel as though I am being washed with water from a gentle stream. With the contamination of the world rinsed off, I feel that the Light within me is able to shine brightly again. The Word is a window cleaner, enabling me to properly reflect Jesus Christ.

By reading a minimum of ten chapters of the Word every day, I could read through the Bible at least twice a year. Since Scripture is His revealed will to me, I wanted to immerse myself in it. The Old Testament, with its strengthening verses, became alive in my heart as I heard the cries of God's people over and over again. His response to such cries filled me with joy. My thoughts and mind were being renewed! My very personality was changing!

Coming out of the pit, the only hope we have for spiritual growth is to feed on the sincere milk of the Word. Soon we will be able to consume the meat of the Word. The Lord is gracious and only feeds us with what we can handle. There is no other way to resurrect and transform a mind than to flood it with the word of God.

In II Peter 1:3-4, we read that, *"He has given us all things that pertain to life and godliness that we might be partakers of the divine nature."* The entrance of the Word of God into your mind and life will enable you to possess this promised gift. We cannot become divine but we can reflect His divine nature through our thoughts and actions.

I began to have a regular routine and was actually quite comfortable with the process that the Lord was working in me. So often, we get too comfortable and are not sensitive to His calling or prompting to move on or to change. In reality, taking control of my life should have meant giving Jesus Christ control and making Him Lord of my life. Going ahead of Him, and sometimes without Him, always teaches me that I am not independent of Him, regardless of how strong He makes me. I need to seek His will in all things!

Chapter 15

Work Camp

In talking with my counselor I asked when I might be moved to one of the work camps. "It would be great," I said, "if I could move to one near my hometown. This would make it less of a hardship for my family to come and visit me."

His response was disappointing. "You have to understand that in dealing with the crime of child abuse, prison authorities are very strict in making their determinations. You probably won't see a camp for at least eighteen months."

I wanted to tell him that this wouldn't help in my efforts to rebuild my family life. But, of course, I didn't. After all, I was the one responsible for nearly destroying my family in the first place. In frustration, I cried out to God, but I did not receive any clear word from Him concerning this situation. All I could do was put my life in His hands and believe that He had a perfect plan for my life and for my family. Because all of my earlier avenues had led to misery and destruction, I refused to turn from the path of the Lord. I prayed, "Jesus, I don't know what to do or even what to pray for anymore. Will you guide my prayers and help me line up to your will? I need

You."

As always, He came to me with signs and wonders, showing me the way to go. There was a central office for the guards in our living units where communications to the inmates were posted on the wall. Inmates who were expecting some notice of change or wanted to check work details would carefully read the communications.

One day, while casually wandering around, I stopped by the office to see if there were any new bulletins. Wading through the tedious notices for shower and sweeping detail, I came to the list of persons scheduled for a urinalysis prior to transfer to work camps or work release. Absentmindedly, I scanned the list, going right past my name. But then my eyes retraced their pathway, and carefully sought out the names. Amazingly, my name was on the list for a transfer to a work camp—the one closest to my home. I was astonished. *How could this be?* I'd only been in prison six months and they were sending me to camp. Hadn't my counselor just told me it would be eighteen months before I could even hope to see any action. *With men, it is impossible, but with God all things are possible.* (Matthew 19:26)

I rushed into my counselor's office and asked him to check on the transfers. He found my name and was, himself, truly amazed. Laughter pealed from my heart as I rushed back to my cell. "Oh my Father, you are so marvelous. When I could not find any direction, you made a way in the wilderness. Please help me never to doubt or fear but, instead, to believe in your wonderful plan for me."

When I called home, my family expressed surprise at my news. It was news which forced them to deal with a number of difficult issues. Each member had very different and personal feelings about the transfer. There was hope, fear, mistrust, doubt and great confusion in their minds. But it was my wife who was faced with making the most difficult decisions — ones which would affect all family members. *Should she continue on with our relationship? Should she continue to visit me with the children? Should she continue to make her husband think that the marriage could continue? Would she be putting her children at risk by allowing this man back into her life?* None of the questions had a clear answer.

Sure I had been acting much differently, but sobriety helps us all behave more acceptably. She had to ask herself, *How permanent are the changes?* Only the Lord could make her see the truth of the rebirth that had taken place within me. Unable to convince her of the change, I asked her to watch and see if Jesus was reflected in my daily walk.

I couldn't tell what Rebecca, my stepdaughter, was thinking. Even though many people reassured her that Jesus had changed me, it did not relieve her anxiety about seeing me face to face once again. In some ways it must have seemed as if people were making light of what had happened to her. But they weren't! They were aware of her pain and the need for me to be held fully responsibile for my actions.

Tommy, my stepson, had many mixed feelings as a new believer. He knew forgiveness was a requirement, and yet he carried within him many deep and serious wounds. *How do I relate to this man*? he asked himself. *What does the Lord expect from me now that my father is obeying the Word of the Lord and walking after the ways of God.* This wonderful boy chose to love me for Jesus' sake even when to do so was painful since he could not reconcile the forgiveness with the hurt. I commend Tommy for his devotion and obedience to Jesus and pray that our relationship now justifies that obedience.

My youngest daughter, Jenny, seemed content to have more contact with "Dad." Every time I saw her she appeared happy, making me totally unaware that by deserting her, I was causing many wounds. Notice I used the word "deserting." For in truth, I willingly deserted the children by the choices I made and the behavior I displayed. They were left unprotected by my sin. I could only trust in the Lord and the Holy Spirit to help me make the necessary amends. The Lord did not fail me in this quest but supplied me with wisdom and discernment to reconcile with my family. The Lord God is so gracious and wonderful. *He daily loads us with benefits.* (Psalms 68:19)

When I told other prisoners, my brothers in Christ, about the transfer, they were happy and excited for me, encouraging me in the Lord and requesting that I continue to pray for them and their needs. I assured them I would and, in fact, I did so for many years.

Chapter 16

The Tests

The next step for me to take was the actual urinalysis. This was a standard procedure. Just give the urine sample and have it analyzed for drug or alcohol content. The morning of the test I forgot that I had to give a specimen and went to the bathroom twice before I realized I needed a sample. When they called my name for the test, I froze. *How could I be so stupid?* Although I tried very hard to go, my body would not cooperate. In desperation, I began gulping what seemed like gallons of water. There's a regulation that requires you to give a specimen within one hour or it is considered a refusal. This means a major write-up. If this happened, it would take at least six months before I could have another chance to be moved to camp.

I know this seems personal and somewhat silly, but our God is so personal that He cares about every small detail of our lives. One of the other problems was that an officer would have to watch you go to be sure that there were no tricks. Sometimes men would try and substitute someone else's specimen to avoid being caught after they had used drugs. With only ten minutes left, I was beginning to sweat. *How could I tell my family that I couldn't go to camp because I couldn't go to the bathroom.* I felt so foolish but I had no other choice than to cry out to the Lord. "Jesus help me go to the bathroom. I want to follow this plan you have for me. Don't let the enemy get a victory here for such a small reason. Please Lord, help me to go." With only moments to spare, I managed to give them a specimen. When it came back clean, I was cleared to be moved to camp. Glory to God for intervening. Remember, if the Lord cares even for the sparrow, then your needs and my needs are important to Jesus Christ. Also, the more you and I include Him in our lives, the more our lives will follow His direction and reflect His personality.

While I basked in the glow of victory with praises of thanks-givings on my lips and in my heart, I temporarily forgot that the enemy never rests. The night before I was to leave for camp, there was a knock on my door. One of the guys I knew came in and sat down. "I just heard that you've been set up for transfer to camp."

"You heard right," I said enthusiastically.

"Great! I bet you feel like celebrating."

"I sure do," I said. "I've been thanking the Lord for His wonderful mercy and grace."

"Well, why don't you stop by my cell tonight and we could have a few drinks to send you off right. I know you used to drink a lot on the streets. Since they've already done the urinalysis, we can kick off this transfer in a big way."

Suspicious that Satan was using this man to bait me, I turned down his offer. "You know I don't like homemade beer."

"Who said anything about beer? Take a look at this." He pulled a bottle of Jack Daniels out of his coat.

Stunned, I looked at the bottle. Because I used to really love whiskey, I knew I had to immediately turn over my thoughts to Jesus Christ. In my mind, I shouted, *Get thee behind me Satan!!! I will not defile myself with this liquor.* Aloud, I said, "I don't intend to throw away the opportunity God has given me to move on."

"But, no one will ever know. You're not being moved until

morning. Come on; you have a reason to celebrate."

"The guards could come in and catch us, and even more importantly, God would know. He has shown me grace and I don't intend to stray. No more being in bondage to alcohol. I've been set free and I'm standing fast."

"But , don't—"

"Please leave my cell and keep your booze to yourself. I don't want it."

He left with a puzzled look on his face and I began thanking God for giving me the backbone to come against this temptation. The following day my move took place as planned!!

Chapter 17

The New Place

It was a typical June day, and the morning broke clear and bright. All inmates being transferred were up at the break of day to get on the bus for the two-and-one-half-hour drive to the camp. I read my Bible most of the way and, in between chapters, praised the Lord for this wonderful opportunity. His plans and timing were so much greater than I could ever have imagined or planned. It was wonderful being back in the mainstream of life—enjoying new scenery, seeing the cars go by, watching people walking around. All of this added to the freedom I had in the Lord Jesus Christ.

My heart skipped a beat as we passed the footbridge that led to my house. Even though it was very early, I hoped to see my family standing there to welcome me home. Of course, this was not realistic. No outside communications, regarding the details of this trip, had been allowed in order to ensure that no one would stop the van to help prisoners escape.

That underpass told me I was almost home—a thought which caused unspeakable joy to well up inside of me. I had no way of knowing that it would actually be two years before I was home because, once again, I had put my plans and desires ahead of God's will for me. He would keep me in prison until I had learned to love Him with all of my heart.

When we stopped at an underground tunnel to drop off some inmates at one of the county jails, I felt very tense. Threatened by the temporary loss of the new freedom I had been experiencing on the freeway, I was relieved when we drove back into the sunlight and continued on toward the camp. In forty-five minutes we would find out what the camp looked like. All of us were nervous and excited, wondering how we would fit in.

Unbelievable, I thought, when I surveyed my new home. *No fences, no walls, no restraining medium surrounding the compound!* This was freedom in the physical sense. After unloading the bus, we were taken into the office and given all the preliminary rules. We were also provided with colored suits to wear so that, if we ran off, we would be easy to spot. The officers wore civilian clothes and only the walkie-talkies in their pockets set them apart from the inmates. The whole atmosphere seemed relaxed. As I praised God for the new surroundings, I thought of the third chapter of Ephesians where He says "*Now unto Him that is able to do exceedingly abundantly above all that we ask or think, according to the power that worketh in us."(Eph 3:20)* Had I given my order for the camp, I would have fallen short of the environment the Lord provided for me.

Located in the midst of a forest clearing, with a nearby brook, and near the foothills to the mountains, it appeared more like a resort than a prison. I was reaping the richness of my divine inheritance and I thanked the Lord over and over again for this wonderful opportunity. Here, I would be able to grow in the Lord with a minimum of distraction. Most of the men worked for the Department of Natural Resources which involved fighting fires in the forests, tree thinning, and tree planting. For someone who had been physically inactive for so long, this was a great prescription for health.

My first order of business was to find the other brothers in the Lord but, after looking around, I realized that there was not one person who had "Christian" stamped on their forehead. I tried to attract Christians by displaying my Bible under my arm as I walked around, or by sitting in the opening of the housing unit and reading passages of Scripture. Sure enough my plan worked! An inmate approached me and made a comment about me reading the Bible. After brief introductions, we began talking.

"I really love the Lord," I said. "You'll find that I spend a lot of time in His Word."

His voice was warm and friendly. "It's great to have another believer here," he said. "Why don't you come to my room and meet a friend of mine.

Agreeing, I followed him to his room. He introduced me to another man. "Mike, this is Carl, one of the new men. And," he said, with enthusiasm, "he's a brother in the Lord."

"That's great. Sit down Carl and have a pop."

"Thanks! I'm glad to find you guys waiting here for me. I knew the Lord wouldn't bring me here without providing fellowship."

And so it was—a new situation and new friends to disciple me in the way of the Lord.

Three times a week, volunteers came to the camp and helped clarify the Word to those of us who were hungry to know more and more of Jesus Christ. I was like a sponge at the time and these volunteers brought practical insights in how to walk the Christian walk.

During this time I was also involved with Alcoholics Anonymous. Since alcohol was a contributing factor in my offenses, the state required that I be involved in AA as well as a drug program offered at the institution. Rather than object because these were not "Christian" programs, I obeyed the authorities over me as the Word commands us. Through these programs, I was given valuable tools for dealing with temptation. I learned about the addiction process, how to identify patterns of behavior, and how to use intervention techniques to break such patterns. In James 1:17, we are told that, "*Every good gift and every perfect gift comes from above.*" All things are subject to the Word of the Lord and the Holy Ghost will help us absorb what is useful and to dispense with the balance.

The faithfulness of the volunteers who took their time and energy and gave so unselfishly gave many of us a greater chance of making it in the outside world. Their actions reinforced the love of the Lord—we began to believe we were important to Him. These volunteers may never realize—until glory—just how many thousands of lives they have affected by their kindness to one of the least of God's children. May God richly bless them all.

One of the first volunteers I met was a pastor who had retired after forty-five years of pastoring a church. He had started the Christian ministry at this particular work camp. However, as so often happens to those used to the battle, when the call came to come to the camp, he responded quickly and began to establish a base for the Lord in the midst of the enemy's camp. Every Sunday night he would come with some of the men from his church and we would sing songs, learn about the Lord, and share about the trials and victories in our lives. These men were so patient with us in hearing about triumphs that probably seemed mundane to them. Truly, they had the gift of graciousness to give us room to grow.

Usually, the pastor would sit with us a few minutes and then he would go over to the men's living unit and talk to the inmates who walked up and down the halls. He would invite them over to the study and encourage them to meet the Lord Jesus Christ. Many of the men called him an old fool, ridiculing him for his belief and desire to care for them. They didn't realize that he was the glory and image of the Lord Jesus Christ and that, before their very eyes, His word was being poured out through this man's heart. The knocking on the door talked about in Revelations 3:20 was taking place through this pastor's outstretched hand who continued to minister to them until he reached eighty years of age.

Although this volunteer is not able to be as active as he once was, he still finds some time to visit the camp and other prisons in the area. I truly thank the Lord for extending His love to me through this man who so widened my understanding of love for the lost. After my release, I visited him at his church where his pastor allowed me to give my testimony before the church body. It was a baptism under fire, but that was the way he was—always seeking to give God the glory—always willing to give—always willing to promote others.

Chapter 18

The Soft Steps

As I began to settle into my new surroundings, the Lord had much work to do within me—and also within my family. For one thing, I had to learn more about the damage I had done to my children and what I could do, through His grace and power, to restore what I had destroyed. Enough time had gone by for them to began communicating, more clearly, about the wounds I had inflicted and about the difficult times they were experiencing in coping with their hurts. The wounds of child abuse are very deep and many lives are affected by the abuse. Even though I was now in the Lord, much work and time would be necessary to help my children lead a normal life. My wife would also need more time to heal after the vicious assaults that were perpetrated by me on her children. The camp was a more conducive place to talk and share with my children. Also, the immediate effects of the trauma had subsided enough to allow the process of healing to begin.

For the next eight to ten months, the number of visits from my family began to increase, allowing us to talk and share as a family. This gift was just one of many that the Lord would give me in His process of restoring the lives of my children and of renewing relationships. Each step seemed so slow but soft steps were necessary to protect those who had been so deeply wounded.

As stated earlier, this was a time of decision for the family. Now that contact was more frequent, they had to face their abuser regularly. Somewhere in their minds they had some memory of who I was as a father and they couldn't reconcile the two images. There was the father who was supposed to have loved them and the vicious person who had abused them. And now they had to add this third person to the equation—this new creature in Christ Jesus. *What was their reaction to be? Were they expected to simply forgive and go on?* Jennie, my four-year-old, seemed to have no real awareness of the damage I had done to her brother and sister. She just knew they had taken her daddy away and that she was happy to see him again. Although her attitude had been the same throughout my incarceration, I later learned that she believed herself responsible for my arrest because she had told the Child Service Worker that I had been in the home. It took much work for her to realize that I was the only one to blame for the separation.

My born-again son was the first to get past the superficial hellos. He was aware that the Lord commands us to forgive others; however, in the instances of abuse, the wounds can be so deep that the victims have trouble letting go of the hurt and pain. The first step in all of these healings is forgiving and allowing the grace of the Lord to come in and minister to the person who has been wounded. My son, to some degree, was able to make this effort and let the Lord do the judging. He was starting to see me as I now was, and the two of us discussed Bible passages and other issues of faith. As he began to show a growing respect for me, he thought, *Could it be that this man who so deeply hurt me has become capable of loving me the way God designed a father to love?* He was willing to give me another chance for a new and deeper relationship to form between us. The Lord showed me that, even in the worst of circumstances, His love and grace can regenerate lives. My son was maturing and overcoming his hurts by the blood of the Lamb. Only through forgiveness was the grace of the Lord allowed to come in to heal and to minister to this wonderful young man.

Rebecca, my oldest daughter, who was the most abused, continued to be the most distant—our problems seemed insurmountable. Love was a shattering experience for her; her trust in others had been crushed. Only a miracle could open her heart to ever again care for others. Her spirit had been wounded. Some call it soul murder. Such wounding makes other relationships very difficult, if not impossible. As victims grow into adulthood, this warped sense of love hounds them, robbing them of the abundant life that is promised to God's children. Somehow, I wanted to deliver her from the lies and messages I had given her about love and loving relationships. Soon I came to hope that, through any means of the Lord, His love could be ministered to this hurting child.

Rebecca is the most precious of children—a delicate and trusting child. "Lord Jesus, spare her the torment from my sin. Renew and regenerate her personality and remove these wounds and memories. Glorify thy name in her life; she is your child."

Slowly a miracle began to bud as the two of us started to have meaningful conversations during our visits. The miracle blossomed as she began to relate to me again as a father. My heart was melting from this miraculous reconciliation. The counseling she had undergone for the past year was helping immensely and the fact that our visits were in a controlled setting was all the better for her. Sexual abuse leaves victims feeling helpless and utterly out of control because of the assaults. Now she had a say of how often and how close our contacts would be.

When she told me that she was beginning to forgive me for the damage, I was elated. Admittedly she was hesitant, but at least the door to healing had been opened. After each visit I would praise the Lord for the opportunity of being near my stepdaughter again and pleaded for the complete restoration of our relationship at a pace that would suit her. Over and over I asked God, "Show me how I can meet her needs. Give me your grace and guidance."

As our relationship improved, I came to recognize the importance of the victim having control over the contact and depth of his/her visits. They have to deal with the internal damage and only they know how comfortable they are with renewed contact with their victimizer. If they never want contact again, then we, as perpetrators, must accept this and do all we can in the Lord to bring the blessings of the Lord into their lives.

After about nine months of visits, the enemy came against us in a way I could not combat. A law was passed that prevented abused children from visiting those who had assaulted them. I was crushed. My stepdaughter was being betrayed again. Here she had been drawing close to me—slowly trusting again—and now I was being pulled out of her life.

Weeping bitterly, Rebecca said she felt "cheated." Her mother related her sorrow to me but I could do nothing. Another wound on top of those just beginning to heal! I could not understand why the Lord allowed this to happen and wanted to take the passing of this law as a personal attack against me and my family. But this was wrong. Often we get so focused on the laws that we lose sight of the work the Lord wants us to do. The purposes of God are perfect and this might well have been the best thing for my stepdaughter. It is the enemy who wants to destroy the families in this country. In our case a family was coming back to wholeness by the power and grace of Jesus Christ. Certainly the enemy could not allow that without putting up a fight; however, God is the Highest Power and does not make mistakes. And so I decided to concentrate on the other relationships in my family, not allowing this ploy of the enemy to render me ineffective in the healing and caring that was needed for my other children.

My wife was very leery of my newfound righteousness. "Is he really different or is he just playing a game to get back at me?" she asked her friends. Yes, there was much doubt and skepticism and this was a difficult obstacle for her to overcome. She had questions to ask of herself. *Can I ever really trust him again? Can I let him be alone with my children again? Won't he just cause greater damage if I give him another chance?* These thoughts were going through her mind as she looked at this seemingly rational man. As the doubts won out, each week there was always an excuse why she could not come to visit me. My brother began to bring the children with him so I could see them. Still, I remained blinded to the truth.

Reconciling myself to the fact that, during my stay in prison, I would not be able to convince Susan that I was different, I hoped that, when I was released, she would see that my conversion to Jesus Christ, and the subsequent changes He made in me, were real. In the meantime, I would just put my trust in the Lord and acknowledge that His ways are perfect. I praised Him for all that went on in my life and for letting me see and endure things that were out of my control.

It is important that my readers realize that I had put this woman through sheer hell. As my wife she suffered from the violence, the drunken assaults, the infidelity and, worst of all, the abuse of her children. The fact that she spoke to me was truly a miracle in itself. I caused her enough pain for a lifetime in just a few short years. "Lord, please destroy all the works of the enemy that I perpetrated. I took this wonderful woman and completely ruined her life. Her ability to love and trust will never be the same unless you do a mighty work in her. My Jesus, the miracle healing that is in me can be in her as well. Please move in Susan's behalf."

If God has placed one of my books in your hands and, if you are an active abuser, I pray that the following words will settle into your mind: "The damage you are doing is so deep and so total that only the miracle of the Lord Jesus Christ can deliver your victim from a lifetime of dysfunction and sorrow. Please, this very moment, seek the help you desire and the freedom for your victims that they so desperately need."

I would like to go back to the day that I had to announce to my parents that I was being sent to prison for child molestation. My therapy group felt that to keep the charges from my parents was to keep a ring of secrecy alive that needed to be destroyed. Their feeling was that the secrecy surrounding the assaults is dangerous and that as many people as possible should know of the deviancy so that others may be protected. I believe this can go to an extreme but the intent is correct. When deviants are abusing, there is a constant web of secrecy, first with the victims and then with others. This must be exposed. Once a person has stopped the actual assaults, then all those who would be affected must be notified of the person's past. This eliminates opportunities to offend, protecting potential victims and providing a safeguard for the abuser.

When I had summoned up the nerve, my wife and I went over to my parent's house to let them know the truth. Nervous and ashamed, I spoke the difficult words. "Mother—Dad—I feel I have to tell you that I've been charged with child abuse for molesting my stepchildren." *There, the words were out. How would they be received?* I didn't have to wait long to find out.

My mother's words were harsh, and revulsion was her first reaction. "Get the hell out of here and never come back again. I hate you. How could you hurt those children? If you just needed sex, why didn't you get a whore? Don't ever talk to us or call us again. I hope they send you away forever."

My father just looked at me without saying a word. I was not aware until much later that his silence was covering the generational sin of abuse that had been in our family. We left and I wept all the way home. The circle of damage had just grown wider by two.

Chapter 19

The Visit

My brother and his family, who lived in Illinois, decided to visit me to find out the truth about the stories they had heard. The fact that I had hurt the children was difficult to accept but, considering the drunken behavior they had witnessed during other visits, they knew it was possible. My confessing left them no doubt about the truth; however, they did question my seemingly miraculous deliverance into the kingdom of Jesus Christ. For years they had witnessed to me about this wonderful Jesus and, if not for them, I might not have known who to turn to that first night in my cell. In fact, during one of my drunken stupors, I'd supposedly said the sinner's prayer over the phone. Perhaps the Lord honored my prayer that day and set my path for deliverance.

Proudly and with excitement, I told my friends about this forthcoming visit from Bob, my SAVED brother. The days seemed to drag and, as the time for their visit grew closer, I had to trust the Lord that I would not get called to a fire. Since it was the fire season, I could get called at any time.

Just three days before my brother was due, a large fire broke out in the northern part of the state. I asked to be excused from this duty; however, since I was a crew member, I had to go. All my begging and pleading was to no avail. After my request was turned down, I walked sadly back to my room, not caring much about anything. Then the Lord spoke to my heart and my somber mood changed. *You will be here for your visit*, He said. *Don't worry*! It didn't seem possible but I was willing to believe.

When I ran back to my room to pack, my roommate looked surprised. "Are you going to the fire?" he asked.

"Yes, they say there's only enough people here to make full crews. There aren't any extra workers in camp because the other two crews are out on another fire."

"But how are you going to get back in time for your brother's visit?"

"Well, the Lord just told me not to worry—that I would be back here in time for the visit. I believe Him," I said simply.

"I sure hope it works out. You know that I'll be praying."

When we arrived at the base camp that Thursday afternoon, we were told to rest because we would have the night shift from 7:00 PM to 7:00 AM. Although we tried to rest, it was impossible because of the 90 degree temperature. The sleeping tent was like a sauna. All night long three crews, working in different places, fought this dangerous fire. Because it was on the cliffs, the smoke and dark made the footing very difficult to secure. That night we cut five miles of fire trail, which is a path three feet wide, down to the bare ground. It is a lot of work but it is one of the methods that stops fires from advancing.

During the night, we spent most of the time right on the fire line, cutting the trail at the fire's edge to keep it from advancing. Because we were concentrating intensely on our work, we weren't thinking about all the possible dangers. Suddenly, I heard a loud thump right next to me. Looking around, I found that a ten foot spar from the top of a tree had landed about one foot from me. "Thank you, Lord, for protecting me," I said, going immediately back to work.

"Carl, I can't believe how lucky you just were," marveled a crew member.

"It wasn't luck. I have the Lord Jesus Christ and He must have sent an angel to protect me."

"I have heard of angels helping people," he said, more to himself than to me.

Later that night I had a wonderful opportunity to witness to him and several of the other crew members about freedom and safety in the Kingdom of God.

The same schedule continued on for the next night as well. On Saturday, I began to get nervous. *Was the Lord really going to get me back on time?* I had to trust that He would. By 2:00 PM, I began to get frantic and, when the work bus left for the fire site about 4:30 PM, there was no sign of my deliverance. My mind searched for excuses to get them to leave me behind. *Let's see. I had ruined my contacts from other fires and now my night vision and depth perception were terrible.* Actually, this would have been very dangerous for someone working at night and in the smoke. However, they did not buy that story and told me to get on the bus for the evening meal.

Soberly, I boarded the bus and plopped down in my seat. *It seemed I would not have the opportunity to rejoice with Bob in my new-found happiness with Jesus.* At that very moment, even before the van door shut, another van drove up with the relief guards. With them came one of the Christian brothers from one of the other work crews. "Hold up for just a moment," they cried. "We need to take Carl back to camp for a special visit."

Sheepishly, I wiped the tears from my eyes. *What a God! What a God! Is there nothing too small for You to do for us? Praise you Lord.* While waiting with these guards for about two hours, I repeatedly witnessed to them about the glory of the Lord and His wondrous mercy. They agreed that, in general, God was good, but right now their lives did not include time for righteousness because of drinking and women. *Fun,* I think they called it. However, to God's glory, one of these men came to the Lord about six months later. *Perhaps my testimony helped him see the beauty of the Lord Jesus Christ.*

Saturday evening, when I entered our room, my roommate didn't seem surprised. "Don't you want to hear about my wonderful miracle—why I'm back on time?"

He smiled. "I know what happened. "When Tim came back from fire fighting, I told him how sad it was for you to have been taken out to the fire just before your visit. I explained that they would only let you come back if someone, who could fight fires and was not on a crew, would volunteer to go in your place. When he said that he wished he could help, I told him he could since I had already put in his name to be a volunteer. After being out for four days, he was tired but he didn't hesitate about filling in for you."

I stared at him in awe. "Thanks for being God's instrument. And Tim—well he is a precious jewel and I can't wait to thank him."

When my brother and sister-in-law arrived the next day, I kept repeating the circumstances that had allowed me to be available for their visit. I couldn't stop praising the Lord. Because I was used to the new me in Jesus Christ, I had forgotten that some people still remembered the man that I had been.

Julie, my sister-in-law was stunned, and I guessed what she was thinking. *Could this really be the same hopeless case my husband has been praying for?*

"Yes," I said out loud. "The Lord, sure enough, could and did save a wretch like me."

My brother was ecstatic, praising God for my deliverance. "All the years of praying and pleading—He heard us—He remembered!"

"Yes, Bob, He remembered, all right and He answered!"

It was a beautiful and memorable day for me, made even

more special because my wife and children had come along with them for the visit. God had, once again, shown that, "*He is able to do exceedingly abundantly above all we think or ask, according to the power that works in us*." (Eph 3:20)

When Bob and Julie returned home, the Lord told each of them independently that they were to move back to our state. He wanted them to help my family. After much prayer, they told their pastor of their intentions. He startled them by saying, "It's just an emotional urge that will pass."

"No, it won't," they insisted. "We've heard from the Lord and we intend to do as He has asked."

I don't recommend disobeying those over you in the Lord; however, if you truly know that He has spoken, then you must be obedient. It is very, very rare that the Lord doesn't confirm His message to you with your spiritual authorities.

By obeying God, my brother and his wife had to move to a strange city, find new jobs, a new home, and a new church body. But they counted the cost of the lives of my wife and children as having greater value than their own comfort.

During the remainder of my stay in prison, my brother and his wife constantly put themselves out for my family. When Tommy began to backslide and became too difficult for his mother to handle, my brother went to pick him up—just an hour before he and another friend planned to run off to California. God's timing is always perfect. My brother took him into his home and raised him as his own son, doing a wonderful job. This young man has become a model of Christian character thanks to his Uncle Bob's wise and caring leading. He still owes much of his growth to this generous man and his wife. I will always love them and thank them for this.

Chapter 20

The Examinations

When the opportunity for me to be transferred to work release came up, I was very excited and surprised since I had only been in prison for about ten months. The administration told me that I would be one of the inmates considered for the December transfer to a large city near my family. I definitely was riding on cloud nine, certain that this was another miracle from our Lord. Before my paperwork could be sent to the State Capitol for approval, I had to be reviewed by their Screening Committee. One requirement for all violent offenders was to undergo a psychiatric evaluation. This was no problem for me as I could just see the astonishment of the psychiatrist when he realized that I had made a complete recovery.

Although prayer and thanksgiving preceded my interview, I had started to take a detour from God's plan for my life by following my own agenda at my pace. The interview was at another prison which housed the criminally insane—persons who could not adjust to normal prison life. It was very eerie and reminded me of another asylum that I had once been in. Everyone spoke slowly and softly and the main means of treatment was medication. Supposedly this was for everyone's best interest.

After being called in by the psychiatrist, we went over the usual preliminaries of who I was, who he was, and why we were there. Much time was spent discussing my crime of child abuse and how I perceived myself and my victims. We then got around to my being transferred back to a place where I might reoffend. I said, "That can never happen because I'm no longer a child abuser. I've been forgiven for that sin and the root of the sin has been destroyed. My feelings for children are normal—father-like, just as I'm supposed to have."

He looked astonished. "Do you mean to tell me that something has all of a sudden healed you of your psychological aberration of child abuse?"

"Yes," I said, "if that means I'm no longer a child abuser, that is exactly what I'm trying to tell you. When I accepted Jesus Christ as my Savior, I was delivered from that sin and all other sin. By following His Word, He has begun to renew my mind so that my damaging thoughts and actions that hurt others have disappeared from my mind."

He was not impressed. "Do you mean to tell me that if you just follow what the Bible says and believe in Jesus Christ, you don't need any help for the crimes you committed and the damage you have done."

"Jesus healed me," I said emphatically. "He really did!"

"So some historical book actually had a positive effect on your deviancy?"

"Doctor," I said, "I know it may seem strange but the Holy Spirit has assured me that I have had a total deliverance. The Lord has given me a new lease on life and I feel wonderful now."

"What about the victims? What about a new life for them?"

"If they will allow the Lord Jesus Christ to reach in and touch their hearts, they can be healed of all their hurts. The Lord is able to deliver them also. It may take some time but, by His grace, all of their wounds can be healed."

The doctor looked very solemn. "I think you have deluded

yourself into thinking that some religion has made this miraculous change in your life. Don't you know how often child molesters use jail-house conversions as a way to get out of treatment and prison. The timing is certainly convenient."

"I—I know this happens—and that it happens often. But in my case, it's true. God knows that my conversion is real—time will prove it to be true."

"You have done some terrible things to these children. Their lives will never be the same. Your God can't change what you did, nor the consequences of your actions. Your victims continue to suffer even though you feel wonderful! No religious writings can change the facts."

"No, but the promises in the Word are true. God changed me and, as I said, He can and will heal my victims."

He looked disturbed. "You seem incapable of facing the truth and I don't see that you have any remorse for your actions. Your religious fantasies make you a danger to society. Believe me, you are a very sick man who needs years of treatment. I cannot recommend your transfer to work release."

I sat there stunned. *Did I hear right? Did he say no? Did he say I was crazy? Who did this guy think he was*? As anger flared, the old man was momentarily brought to life. I was on the verge of some tirade, ready to vent all my anger and disappointment on this pawn of the state. *How dare he question the Lord Jesus Christ and His work in me?* Suddenly a calm came over me and I felt the presence of the Lord who told me, *It will be okay.* Slowly I got up from my chair, thanked him for his time, and told him I looked forward to having his favorable report soon.

People will always question the work of the Lord because they cannot fathom how such dramatic changes are possible without man's wisdom being involved. This man was questioning the sincerity of my conversion and, because of his previous experiences with inmates, I understood the reason why. He had to think about the welfare of children. *But,* I thought, *my faithfulness to Jesus over a long period of time will show him the truth.*

Arriving back at the work camp, I tried to deal with my feelings of disappointment. And then Satan took advantage of the moment and filled my thoughts with doubts. *Maybe I really was not healed. Maybe I'm just fooling myself. This Jesus thing could be just another of the many avenues I had tried in search of some meaning. Maybe I was still dangerous to the public in general and to my children specifically. Maybe I should be kept in prison.* Immediately, I received assurance from the Lord that His work was real. Also, the confidence of my Christian friends was instrumental in helping me overcome this attack. After a few days passed, I came to grips with the fact that the spiritual truths of the Lord are not readily discernible by those who do not believe. Of course, those who have been delivered from severe sin need to learn new paths of behavior, but to dismiss God's miraculous healing is wrong. In First Corinthians 2:14 , we read, "*But the natural man does not receive the things of the Spirit of God, for they are foolishness to him; nor can he know them, because they are spiritually discerned.*"

It has been ten years since that interview and I am still planted firmly in the bosom of the Lord Jesus Christ. In fact, through His grace, I have been a blessing to many children and a danger to none. My God is an awesome God. Years later, when I got a copy of this doctor's report, I learned that he had recommended for me to be transferred from the work camp to a maximum security prison in our state. He also recommended that I should be kept under a strict counseling and monitoring regimen that would cost approximately $2000.00 per month. He did not, however, suggest who should pay for such treatment. The report further stated that I should have no more visits from my children and that I should refrain from all future contact with them. His final recommendation was to have me serve the rest of the ten years before I was released.

Even though I didn't see this report at the time, I knew that some problems would probably come from this man's evaluation. With much prayer I asked the Lord for direction. Through my brother, who was aware of this encounter, I met a Christian psychiatrist who was willing to evaluate me. Within a short time, the interview was set up and I was taken to see him. After going through all the same preliminaries, the doctor stopped and said, "I want us to pray before we begin, asking the light of the Lord to cover all that is done and said here today."

Nodding in agreement, I commented. "I want God as my witness since He is the one who changed me."

"Lord," he said, "we are here before you this day to examine Your work in this man. Show us what roads or avenues are open and needed in order to help him understand his past sins. Use him to bring about restoration to those who have been hurt."

After two hours I left this man's office, having told him the same things that I had shared with the prison psychiatrist. My testimony never changes. "I was blind and now I see by the grace of the Lord Jesus Christ." However, I could not read the doctor or sense his attitude. The guard asked me how I thought I'd done.

"I don't know, he didn't say much and I think it's better not to speculate."

"You're right. There's no sense in guessing. Besides, you'll get the report soon."

"It's all in the Lord's hands now."

As it turned out, he gave me a solid report in regard to my understanding of my crimes and their consequences to the victims. He described my earnest desire to help them become whole again, and my willingness to do whatever was necessary to prove that my healing was permanent.

The end result of these two reports was that the administration could not make a determination about my qualifications.

This was, however, not communicated to me and, when I asked my counselor how the progress of my transfer request was going, I was told that the committee had approved it and sent it on to the State Capitol for approval. This information led me to encourage my family that I might be in work release before Christmas of that year. Everyone was excited. The obvious changes in my behavior and the prospect of me being home soon, gave my wife a renewed sense of hope. Knowing that transfers could take as long as three months and that this would cut it close for Christmas, I prayed daily for news.

"Oh, God, please give me favor in the capitol with those who are over my case." The tension began to mount in me as November passed into December. Since I was now working in the camp school, I didn't have to go out to the forest and this gave me more time to inquire about my transfer. Always, I was told to be patient because the answer could come any day. As December rolled on I began to sweat. I know that the Lord is never late, but sometimes He makes me nervous when he delivers my desired goal at the last moment.

Finally, just one week before Christmas, I went to the head of the Review Committee and asked if he would call the capitol and see if there was a hold on my paperwork. Astonished, he said. "Your paperwork never left the camp. We turned you down three months ago. I'm surprised your counselor didn't tell you that. You'll have to wait until February for the new superintendent to resubmit your plans. This means you won't be able to transfer for at least six more months."

My hopes and dreams were shattered. Without responding, I meekly turned and walked back to my room. *How could this be? How could the Lord lead me on this way?* I realized that I had put myself on this roller coaster ride by going ahead of God. Instead of listening for confirmation, I chose to forget the reality of God's will and to expect a miracle. Of course, I believe in miracles from the Lord, but this expected miracle was one of my desire and making. The counselor had grossly misled me and, although it took awhile for me to forgive him, I learned patience from this episode. But it was going to be very difficult to tell my family that I wouldn't be home for Christmas.

Chapter 21

The Prodigal Son

On December 19th my family visited me, bringing with them a couple of early Christmas presents. After our usual hellos and hugs, my wife said, "The rest of your presents are waiting for you at home."

I don't want to tell her, I thought. *I just can't tell her!* Finally, I looked at her, murmured a quick prayer, and began. "I have some disappointing news. It seems the Review Committee never approved my papers. It'll be at least six months before I come home."

At first she stared blankly at me which made me very nervous. "I didn't mean to mislead you—it wasn't my fault. The information given to . . ."

"Don't," she said, very softly. "I don't want to know what went wrong. Just please don't tell me ever again about the possibility of you coming home. I can't take the hurt and disappointment."

I looked helplessly at the children. They seemed sad and somewhat confused, but they weren't hurting like their mother. I believe this was the turning point in our relationship—the moment she gave up on us. Even though I had no control over the decision, I was the focal point of another hurt for her. The remaining time of the visit was very somber. Although we exchanged a few gifts and appeared friendly, something died between us that day. Very quietly my family left, the vision of restoration quickly fading. I sensed, as I waved good-bye, that I was also saying good-bye to my vision of restoration.

It was three months before I saw the children again and my wife didn't come until a month later. The hope I still harbored was held together by the slimmest of threads—threads which Satan was determined to break. He was out to destroy my entire family, first attacking me and now my wife. The rest of the holidays were very depressing for me, and I waded through the New Year's weekend without saying much to the Lord. Though I didn't say so out loud, I felt that He had let me down. There was a seed of bitterness planted in my heart because I did not get my way.

Once again, I had gone ahead of God, making my own plans and planning my agenda. Even though I acknowledged this and realized that I needed to learn more about patience, I distanced myself from Him. The next three months passed very slowly. Methodically, I read the Bible every day, prayed every evening, and attended all the Bible studies. Outwardly, I gave the appearance that everything was fine; however, the seeds of bitterness were growing, yielding discontentment and an empty feeling. I tried to praise the Lord for all things but my spirit never came into agreement with my words. For three months my walk was as dry as the valley of bones in Ezekiel 16. And just like those bones, only the Lord could put life back into me.

One March evening I was the only inmate in attendance at the Tuesday night Bible study which was taught by a college student. Ken, the leader of the group, brought one of his friends named Larry with him that night. The three of us sat around and made small talk for the first few minutes. " How are you? Fine and You? Blah, blah, blah."

My body was there but I was definitely absent in spirit. Finally, Ken looked at me and said, "Carl, is there something bothering you? You seem troubled."

"No," I said. "Nothing's wrong." Because I had been carrying this bitterness for so long, I no longer felt its weight and didn't realize that it had begun to change my countenance.

Ken was insistent. "I really feel that something is bothering you. Don't you want to talk about it?"

"No, I'm telling you that there's nothing to talk about." After a few moments of uncomfortable silence, we just stared at one another. Then, I felt the presence of the Lord and knew I had to talk.

"Yes, I do have something to talk about. It's—well, I'm angry that the Lord didn't allow me to go home at Christmas. I was really counting on being home. He let me down."

"Do you think God was trying to be unfair to you?"

"Yes," I said, looking down at the floor. "I do."

"Are you telling me that if God doesn't do what you want Him to do, you won't serve Him? Is this all it takes to separate you from His love? You seem like a spoiled little kid who didn't get his way and is going to pout until someone feels sorry for him. Is this the image you want to project as a Christian?"

Embarrassed, I didn't reply, but I knew that he had spoken the truth. *How easily I had turned my back on the Lord! Was my love for Him conditional ? Did it go away whenever I had my feelings hurt?* I had indeed been childish by allowing the bitterness to crowd out all the wonderful things He had done for me. He loved me unconditionally—it didn't matter how many times I failed Him. *Why hadn't I responded in the same way?*

Ken knew he had my attention. "I feel that your faith and walk with the Lord is tied to your release date. If He doesn't get you out of prison according to your schedule, you won't serve Him."

There was no way I could deny what he was saying, but his words hurt. The truth is often painful and yet, in that pain, there is always freedom. At last I was ready to acknowledge my bitterness! For the next half hour these two men prayed for me. They led me in prayer, declaring my repentance and helping me to release the unforgiveness and hurt for what I felt the Lord had done to me. Certainly, the Lord did not need my forgiveness; however, I did need to release Him from owing me anything. The Holy Spirit welcomed me back into the arms of the Lord who had never left me or stopped loving me.

After the volunteers left, I returned to my cell, knelt before God, and reiterated my repentance. His joy began to flood my spirit, bringing me back to the fullness of my Christian walk. Realizing that, while wallowing in self-pity, I had neglected my prison ministry, I went to my hurting Christian brothers and asked for their forgiveness. A new zeal flooded over me and I was even hungrier to study His Word. Our Lord is so gracious. Even though, after my tantrum, I didn't deserve to be brought into His goodness, my Heavenly Father was there waiting for His prodigal son.

Chapter 22

The Mind is the First Battlefield

The Christian psychiatrist who had evaluated me wrote a letter asking if it were possible for me to come to his office on a regular basis for treatment. Knowing that I would be required to have treatment after I was released, I was encouraged that the doctor was willing to help me. *But, how willing would the state be in allowing me to go to treatment while I was still in the camp?* After considering the request, the administration agreed to provide a guard to escort me once a month for two-hour sessions. The cost, which my parents graciously paid, was $120.00 per month. I was excited to receive the treatment, knowing it would not only help me, but that this Godly man would make me aware of the needs and requirements of my children and wife. He would increase my skills to help in their recovery. This was a true blessing that the Lord had engineered for me. It was a gateway to my family being healed.

Knowing that it was unusual for prison authorities to agree to transport me to the counselor at their cost, I thanked God for his favor over those in authority. I was beginning to feel like Joseph.

In the first session, we spent two hours recounting my side of the abusive episodes. Admitting that, in the past, I had shown no concern for the feelings of my stepchildren was an important step. I also accepted total responsibility for the attacks and could, at this point, only hope to minister, as they would allow, to help in their restoration and recovery. I knew that they could find wholeness in Jesus Christ. I also had to declare that, because of the work of the Lord already in me, there would never again be danger of my abusing children. In my heart I knew I was free of this sin and yet, the deceitfulness of sin made me wary even of myself. I asked the Lord to reveal anything in me that still would give Satan a foothold. Only by relying on the strength of my Lord would I stay out of the sexual sins that had plagued me.

The doctor wanted me to admit my guilt without trying to minimize the damage that I had done to my victims. Truthfully, I told him that Jesus Christ was alive in me. This was the starting point and led to the next step which was to acknowledge that Satan would not rest in his attempts to accuse and tempt me at every turn. Using God's Word, I learned how to resist him. I became steeled in using Scripture for each attack, thereby declaring and rebuking the enemy when thoughts or situations occurred that were not of the Lord.

As soon as a temptation came, especially regarding old actions and thoughts, I cried out the name of Jesus and sought His help. Never will I try to rationalize it away or think my way through it; instead, I immediately go to the Word of the Lord for deliverance. The most important thing I learned was not to waste one moment trying to battle my thoughts. The longer one fights such temptations, the longer they stay with you. Since the enemy had enough ammunition from my past, I did not need to help him by dwelling on old sins. Even to this day, when the enemy brings accusations against me, I immediately cast out the thoughts in the name of Jesus and acknowledge that I belong to Him. Success comes from fleeing temptation, not wrestling with it.

When a person has been delivered from pornography and

sexual deviancy, it is imperative that no place is given to the devil through the mind. The wickedness that I concocted all started with perverse thinking which eventually became actions. The Lord truly renewed my mind through the Word but the enemy is relentless and unceasing in his attack against the mind. Hold fast to this tenet. The mind is the first battlefield. Keep thoughts focused on the things of the Lord and be ready at all times to repel the enemy. Keep all evil from your eyes. Remember it is easier to stay out than get out.

Through counseling, I began to gain strength against the enemy. And, praise God, the more I rebuked him, the weaker he became in his attacks. He began making sneak attacks when I was relaxed and not on alert. The Lord was developing a willingness in me to stand against these areas of sin.

The next month I explained how much better the battle had been going. The doctor was pleased and took me to the next step. He went to his library shelf and returned with three books for me to read; all three dealt with stories of women and children who had been abused.

"I want you to learn from their own lips what the attacks felt like," he said. "I want you to know their hurt so you can begin to understand the hurt that your children have suffered."

The pages of the books ripped my heart apart. The words of victims became ingrained in my mind and increased my determination to help my children be healed of their wounds. I read all three of the books three times, trying to understand the depths of the wounds that I had caused. Although it was not going to be easy, I was determined to see my children through recovery. This would have to be done without answering back or trying to justify anything. For once, they would be in total control, calling the shots as to if and when we would spend time together. They also determined if and when there would be appropriate hugs. I begged God for the strength to rebuild the ruins I had created. The Lord searched my heart and gave His blessing to proceed.

The time in prison was actually helpful for the children since we visited in a controlled and safe environment. This slow beginning allowed them to move at their own pace. Sometimes I had to be reminded that it was my children's right to allow, or not allow, me to be a part of their lives. The Lord, through His mercy, was giving me the tools I would need to rebuild the ruins.

Each month the counseling revealed more about myself and the task ahead of me. The doctor always kept our work under the Lord's authority, which was the only way for me to advance. The Holy Spirit was doing a work in me. It was a great threesome. I was learning, the doctor was leading, and the Holy Spirit was revealing. Through our talks I was kept on course, reigned in when necessary, and given the green light when appropriate. Always we kept sight of the concern of others that I might reoffend. It was important that I be completely honest if any temptations were occurring that I was not overcoming. Progress demanded that there could be no hidden sins. The Holy Spirit revealed my problems to the doctor. The light of the Lord is pure.

We covered possible situations that might be problems and searched my heart to see what my reactions would be. I have found that going over possible situations and making the right decisions beforehand makes the actual decision almost second nature. I like to rehearse the right ways of the Lord. When temptation strikes, pre-armed with the Word of the Lord, I am ready at all times to do what is right in His sight.

Inwardly, the Holy Spirit made me conscious of the fact that the Lord had done a finished work in me. I was no longer a child abuser! His redeeming work and also the opportunity to be trained in healing was complete proof that my old man had died. The Word truly renews the mind, body, soul, and emotions. The natural love I had for children returned. The desire to help others was reborn in me. Looking out for the needs of others was utmost in my mind and thoughts. It seemed even my memory was being renewed. No longer dwelling on former things, I was to remember His forgiveness and renewing work. Through the work of the Holy Spirit and treatment, I was becoming a whole person again, understanding my ability to stand in Christ and to rebuke the lies of the enemy. His accusations were aimed toward my weaknesses. "*You'll never be able to resist temptations when you get out. You will never be able to stay in Jesus. You have never stuck to anything in all of your life. You will not stay in this phony Christian life.*" The slivers of the lying fabric of the enemy cannot be woven if we listen to the Spirit of Truth and get direction from the Lord of Light. Because of His mercy, my past can now serve as a witness to the marvelous ability of the blood of Jesus to transform even the worst of deviants.

One of the most important safeguards that the doctor provided me with is that of accountability. It is necessary for me to always be aware of my situation and of those around me. I know that the Lord has changed me and that I am no longer a danger to children; however, others might not be so sure or understanding. Also, in the event that I am accused of abuse, I would need proof of my innocence. Therefore, I look at every situation as a snare from the enemy. When I find myself alone in a room with children, I either leave the room or make sure that doors are open so others have access. Because children are very playful and like to climb on adults, I have to be stern with them to keep them off of me. Even in the presence of their parents, I make every effort to eliminate contact. Again, I assert the fact that I am not an abuser now, but the danger of accusation and reproach cannot be ignored. It is crucial to express the truth of our past so that we are no longer living a life of deception. No more secrecy! As humbling as it is, I have to be prepared to make the parents of children I am in contact with aware of my reason for being in prison. They have a right to decide if they wish to have contact with an ex-offender. In counseling sessions, I deliberately used the worse case scenarios, preparing myself for any and all dangerous situations.

The meetings went on for six months with the doctor giving me "homework" to do between sessions. I learned about the empathy that would help me to understand my part in hurting others and the wounds that they would have to be healed from. This counselor greatly helped with my recovery by always insisting that I walk in the truth and accept responsibility for my sins. Most of all, he helped me to move toward wholeness through the help and teaching of the Holy Spirit. May the Lord continue to bless his ministry as he continues to help many hurting people.

Chapter 23

Founded in the Rock

In my continuing effort to grow spiritually, I took many correspondence courses which enabled me to better understand the Word as it related to my everyday life. Some new things were also happening. My Christian roommate was leaving and another person would be moving in with me. As you can imagine, this was an exciting time for me. Also, a court decision had been reached by the State Supreme Court that would possibly reduce my sentence. Once again the overwhelming joy of the Lord was surrounding me. It seemed as if everything was going my way; however, I was becoming in love with His presents and losing sight of how much I needed His presence. The roommate I had for most of the first year was a brother named Robert. He had a marvelous testimony of the Lord working in his marriage. When he went to prison for his second term, his wife left the state and filed for divorce. One day, as we prayed about his situation, prison officials called his name for a visit. His wife had been told by the Lord to come back and wait for her husband. She obeyed and they resumed their relationship. This was encouraging and reminded me that the Lord could restore my marriage, too.

Robert had been an alcoholic. One day, as we sat in our

room sharing thoughts and beliefs, I told him that since the Lord had delivered me from alcoholism, I felt I could drink again when I was out of prison. Since I was forgiven for all my sins and healed of all my diseases, I reasoned that I must be cured from my alcoholism. It made sense to me.

Robert bolted upright. "That is a lie from the pit of hell! Don't you know that once you've been delivered from bondage, the Lord teaches us not to be entangled with it again? My thoughts were similar to yours the first time I got out of prison. And so I drank! And then suddenly I was in the same sin situation that led me my arrest. The alcohol numbed my mind and I lost my ability to do what was right in the Lord. Blinded to the power of the Lord, I invited the enemy into my life—and he came."

It was obvious that he was sincere. "I—thank you for being so honest with me. The things you said, well, I needed to hear them. It's amazing how Satan sneaks in with his lies!"

"I wanted you to learn from my experience."

"I have, brother. The Lord used you to save me from an untruth—one that could have wiped me out Thank you for obeying Him."

Usually, we were allowed to choose our own roommates since this seemed to curtail the arguing. I asked Tim. He was the person who had taken my place in the fire, allowing me to visit with my brother Bob.

He did not hesitate. "I'd be glad to share quarters with you."

Once he was settled in, the two of us became close friends, encouraging one another in our Christian walk. Tim was . . . well, he was an overcomer of adversity, getting his strength and knowledge from spending eight hours a day reading Scripture. An avid student of the Word, he took correspondence courses and read all the Christian literature he could get his hands on. Totally convinced of the reality of God, he wanted to share his faith with others. He felt led to teach and firm up the body to stand on the Word of the Lord.

Tim's studying made me feel inadequate, challenging me to increase my own time in the Word. Determined to focus on the Lord, I began to increase my study time. There was more studying and less extracurricular activities such as television, card playing, and sports.

Tim's presence was of great benefit to me. We would spend hours just sharing our insights and discussing scripture. In a sense our room became a chapel where other brothers could seek us for counseling and prayer. Similar to David and Jonathan, we became quite a ministry team. I thank the Lord for giving me such a good friend. He helped me when I was down and I helped him when he was down. Praise God we weren't both having problems at the same time.

When I got the notice from the state that my sentence had been reduced by one year, I couldn't believe it. According to the way the terms run in our state, this meant I was now past my release date. They were going to have to let me go. Even with the slowness of the state, I knew that I would be home in only a few months. The Lord was so gracious. How did I, a sinner, ever deserve such wonderful treatment? I felt like His favorite son. Once again He was directing my path and, once again, I began to run with the graciousness of the Lord. Soon I would be out of prison and my family would be restored. Everything would be perfect! Wrong!

It was now May and I had a parole hearing scheduled for August. In light of the new sentence reduction, I felt sure they would move up my hearing and so I went to my counselor and requested that he make this an official request. He agreed that he would try for the next hearing which was the beginning of July. That wasn't great but still better than my scheduled date in late August. A few days later, we received word back that the date could not be changed since hearings were set up many months in advance. Disappointed and upset, I let him and the Lord know that I was not pleased with the delay. At this point

I should have begun to realize that what I thought was going to happen wasn't going to happen.

When I calmed down I convinced myself that the Lord was working a miracle for me. Once again I was full of joy—but the joy was in something I wanted to happen—not in Jesus. Baseball, Bible studies, work, and other activities made the time go by very quickly and, as my hearing date approached, I spent much time thanking the Lord and promising to praise Him regardless of their decision. The parole plan I submitted was made according to their directions and detailed where I would go, the treatment program I would be in, and the pursuing of employment which would utilize my accounting degree.

On the date of the hearing, I was accompanied by a substitute counselor since mine had been transferred just a week earlier. He really didn't know me and was of little help during the session. After reviewing my papers and proposed plan for parole they said, "We are very disturbed by this report we have in your files from the state psychiatrist. It is very unfavorable to you. There seems to be some fear here that you are on the verge of reoffending. You must realize our position in having to protect the public."

Trying to calm myself, I spoke, "Didn't you read the report by the other doctor? He says I have been making great progress and with continued treatment would be of no risk to the community."

"Yes, we have read his report but we have to give more credence to our own doctors. We cannot make a decision today regarding your release."

My voice level raised, "Do you realize I am already four months past my release date? It is illegal to hold me any longer. I demand that you set my date for parole." Of course, this was the wrong thing to say. The Lord says to agree with your adversary while you are in the way lest he deliver you to prison and you will not come out until you have paid the very last whit. (Mt. 5:25)

"You are in no position to demand anything. You are guilty of a serious offense and we will take every precaution allotted us by the law to ensure public safety. Within sixty days you will have our decision." The spokesman cleared his throat authoritatively. "And now, you are dismissed."

Back in my cell, I was still steaming. *How dare they? Don't they know how much God has changed me? Don't they know how much I have progressed through treatment?* I yelled at the Lord. "How could you have let me down? Why didn't you step forward to help me?" Hearing nothing from Him, I began, once again, to wallow in self-pity. *Everything I planned is ruined. I can't believe this has happened to me.*

I called Bob and told him how the Board had stuck it to me. "I have had it with this waiting on the Lord stuff," I said.

There was a long pause. "Carl," he said, "You have to calm down. There's no way you could hear from God when you're in this state."

Not getting the sympathy I wanted, I abruptly said good-bye, stomped down the hall, went into my room, and threw myself on the bunk.

I was still furious. *How could the Lord not do what I wanted?*

As soon as I hung up, my brother got on his prayer chain and within minutes the whole church was praying for me. The conviction of the Holy Spirit fell on me like a blanket. Godly sorrow bubbled up in me as I heard the echo of my own voice. *Everything I have planned. Not God but me. My plans, my purposes and my direction.* I had forgotten about His direction and His purposes and His work for me in His time. Oh, Lord how easily I turn against you when things don't go my way. *What will it take for me to finally stand up and love You for You and not for what You can do for me?* I quickly repented and could feel His peace and joy flooding me.

When I called my brother back and asked his forgiveness, I

told him that he would not hear any more outbursts from me. He assured me I was forgiven and encouraged me to hold on to the Lord. "God is working His perfect will in you."

Sheepishly, I said, "I know He—I know I can trust Him with my life. This time I've learned my lesson." No longer was I going to put God in a box so that He had to perform for me. I was going to wait on Him and rejoice in all that He brought my way. No more complaining from me. No sireee.

Two months later I heard from the Parole Board and was told that I had to submit plans for parole all over again. This was disappointing since it usually took three months from start to finish. In the middle of the night, we had a fire drill. It was very cold and there was snow on the ground. When one of the younger inmates threw a snowball and some of the flakes landed on me, because of my bad attitude, I turned around and swore at him. My friends were shocked at what came out of my mouth. The young man replied in a challenging fashion and I was ready to test him there in the snow. My friends pulled me away and I thought the incident was over.

The next day the Holy Spirit began to press me to apologize to this individual. However, my pride was in control and I refused to listen to His prompting. All day He prompted me but I continued to resist. The next day the message was unmistakable. *Apologize*! By the third day I still had not apologized, although I was beginning to chafe under His calling. I went to breakfast and was standing in line with the others. Although I didn't notice anything wrong, one of the men later told me that the young man had intended to stab me, but a guard had walked in and ruined his plans. Now I knew why the Holy Spirit was prompting me—it was for my own safety. Yet even more, it was a matter of obedience. I swallowed my pride and the next opportunity I had, I went up to the young man and apologized. He was somewhat stunned but understood when I told him I had been upset over a parole hearing decision. We actually began working on the same crew which provided me an avenue of witnessing. I also learned the necessity of quickly obeying the Holy Spirit.

My parents were too sick to have me come to live with them and my wife had decided not to have me move back home, so my only avenue for parole was to live with my brother Bob. He agreed that I could come to his two-bedroom apartment where he lived with his wife, their son and my stepson. It was going to be crowded for a while but I figured I could get a job and move out in a few months. The investigation went fast and by the end of October they were ready to make a decision.

The parole officer came to visit me, saying he liked to meet his caseload before they came into the community. He looked over my records and told me that, if it were up to him, I would never get out again. "If I even suspect you are guilty of violating one of my rules, I will send you back to prison so fast your head will swim. And—I'll make sure you never get out again."

I swallowed nervously. *Is this what I need, Lord, to ensure I will never offend again? I'm willing to do whatever is necessary. This seems harsh but I'm prepared to comply.* The Lord then showed me that, since the Parole Board had only given me three requirements, I should question the validity of there being so many more. I took my copy of the requirements to my counselor and he wired them to the state capital. The next day they overturned the parole officer's requirements and directed him to follow the three that they had suggested. He was furious.

On the day that he had to submit his report, he was called by my sister-in-law who told him that she did not want me to come to their home. She was afraid for her son's safety. Bob called him right back and said that they had resolved their differences and that I could live with them. Then the parole officer filed a report turning my parole plan down because of dissension in the home. I was, once again, at a loss to understand what the Lord was doing. In speaking with my brother on the phone, I told him the next time that he heard from me I would be in Canada. "I never had this much trouble when I served Satan," I screamed.

Retreating to my room, I wept for my lack of trust. Oh Lord Jesus Christ, once again, at adversity's first call I ran for cover. "Oh, Jesus, will you forgive me again." I murmured. "I love You—I truly love You. If I do the rest of my ten years, then I will do it with joy. I belong to You and I am through wavering at every storm. I am founded in the Rock and I will not be moved."

When I got Bob on the line, I felt calm and peaceful. "I'm sorry for my latest outburst. Please know that it won't happen again and that I am in the capable hands of the Lord Jesus. I have finally reached the point of loving my Savior as my Lord. I want His will for my life."

"Praise God," my brother replied. "He has done some deep work in you."

One night I was playing basketball when I got hit in the face with the ball. To be exact, the ball struck my eye socket perfectly, damaging my right eye. I fell to the ground crying out to the Lord. When the office staff looked at the eye, the swelling had begun and, within fifteen minutes, I lost my vision. The staff was nervous and decided that the best option was to take me to the nearest hospital. Dressed in orange overalls so that I wouldn't try to escape, I was taken to the hospital and examined. The doctor gave me some medication to control the pain and said that I should see a specialist in the morning.

Once again, I was dressed in the orange overalls before being sent to the city. Many of the guards were upset at this, saying that I was a model inmate and that wearing such attire in the city would be humiliating. Nevertheless, the duty officer sent me out dressed like a pumpkin. The eye doctor took care of the damage and I was sent back to the camp with instructions to take off a week to allow for healing. During all of this time, I was looking for an opportunity to share the gospel since I believed the Lord had allowed my injury for a reason.

Although there was no one in the waiting room of the hospital or doctor's office that I witnessed to, on the way home the woman guard who was driving me began to tell me how she used to be in the Lord. She'd been in a near-fatal accident and was at death's door when she felt a resurgence in her body and awoke to see Jesus leaving her room. I was stunned. Such a dramatic testimony.

"How could you walk away from the Lord after something like this?"

She looked at me sadly. "I went to many different churches and all of them were more concerned with fashion and position than sharing the love of Jesus Christ. After awhile, I just gave up."

This was my opportunity to talk about a personal commitment and relationship with Jesus Christ. For an hour we shared back and forth about how wonderful it is to be in Jesus, closely and personally. I encouraged her to look to Jesus first and foremost because people, Christian or not, will let you down. She agreed to try again, keeping her eyes on the Lord and not on the church people. If we all do this, we shall never be offended.

Chapter 24

Work Release

Thanksgiving and Christmas went by uneventfully. The children had been coming with my brother to visit me and our relationships were gradually improving. The freedom developing between me and my son allowed us to hug each other and affirm our love in a healthy way. My youngest daughter and I seemed to relate as though I had never been gone. The Lord was truly restoring the fruit of my wasted years. In Joel 2:25, He tells us that, *"I will restore all the years the locusts have eaten."* I could see this coming to pass before my eyes. The Word of the Lord is so true and perfect and brings light to the simple.

During one of Bob's visits, I commented. "It is going to be wonderful when I'm out of here and I can be with Susan again."

He stared at me intensely. "Don't you think it's a little strange that she hasn't come to visit you for over three months and that she never writes you or accepts your calls?"

"She—she just needs some space," I offered.

"Hasn't it occurred to you that she's left you and doesn't want you to come home to her?"

I tried to sound confident. "She'll change her mind when I get home."

My son didn't agree. "Dad, there's another man living at

home with Mom. She doesn't want you back."

When the words came from him, I realized I could no longer ignore the truth. Though it was like a cold slap in the face, it was reality. My marriage was shattered and it seemed that restoring it was not part of God's plan. Though facing the truth had wounded me, the presence and comfort of the Lord kept me from depression. Having already spent too much time in self-pity, I couldn't sink back into that pit. My eyes were always open, watching for opportunities to minister to others through prayer and Biblical counseling. In serving the Lord, I found the freedom and peace I needed to get through my personal loss. His grace made the difference in helping me accept all that came my way. This was not the last tragedy or giant hurdle that I faced but no longer did I distance myself from God during such times.

When the dearest personal relationships are removed from our lives, can we still be in love with the One who loves us the most. As it turned out, it may be that the Lord was saving me from a snare that would have brought me back into alcoholic bondage. So often in relationships where one of the addicts has been cleaned up, the other stays in bondage and drags the "recovered" person back into the pit of misery and destruction. *Perhaps this would have happened to me if my wife had taken me back.* Again, the wonder of God's wisdom in seeing the whole picture, and not just each small step, truly amazes me. Each new revelation of deliverance made me more and more aware that I could totally trust in His direction and plan for my life.

That year, at the New Year's Eve party, which was held in the gymnasium, I was the dealer for blackjack. Everyone used paper money to gamble with and whoever had enough left at the end of the night was able to buy, or rather bid, for mystery gifts. The gifts ranged from money on the books to gag items such as a pair of pantyhose. To my surprise, I was having a good time. The joy of the Lord was beaming from my face and I was complimented for the banter and fun I provided for the contestants. It was a wonderful opportunity to let the inmates know that the joy I felt was because of the love of the Lord. They were as lonely and hurt as I had been in previous holidays. How desperately I wanted them to understand that, in Jesus, there are no terrible situations, at least none that we have to face alone. I said what I could, keeping the name of the Lord before them.

It was then the Lord revealed to me that it was time to leave the camp and move on toward release. I still had not received word from our State Correction's Office as to when that would be. The Lord pressed me to contront the superintendent about the move.

As I was coming from work, I saw him heading toward the administration building. "Sir, Sir,." I said.

"Yes, Carl."

I chose my words very carefully. "I know you are a Christian and that you believe in the Holy Spirit."

"Yes, I am and I do!"

"Well, the Lord has revealed that it is time for me to be let go. I only ask that you seek the Lord and see if He doesn't tell you the same thing."

He stared at me with searching eyes. "I'll pray and then get back to you."

The next day he called me into his office. "Carl, I prayed last night and the Lord revealed to me that I should let you go. This week I'll contact the State Correction's Office and authorize your release."

Praising God, I said, "Thank you, Sir. I'll be waiting for official notification."

A few weeks later, I received a call to go to the Administration Building. Since I had been working for the teacher and often went to the building, I didn't give any particular significance to the request. I strolled over and saw my counselor who promptly informed me that in just two weeks I would be going to work release. Although I was very pleased, I did not feel the excitement one might have expected. Having truly reached the place in my Christian walk where I totally placed my faith in Christ and His plan for me, my life had become very fulfilling. Of course I wanted to go home, but there was no euphoria or extreme feeling of release. The Son had already made me free. The best that the state could do was to confirm what my God had already done. Thanking Him and giving Him the glory, I went back to work.

I shared the news with the brothers and they were all very happy that God was moving me along in His plan for my life. The volunteers were happy also and wished me well. One of the couples who ministered at the facility asked me to exchange addresses and telephone numbers with them. I was flattered and considered the request to be a vote of confidence as people in prison can quickly go the wrong direction once they are free. These people were sticking their necks out to assist a brother in the Lord and I appreciated their merciful hearts. Over the months that I had spent in the work camp, this couple had stood out above many of the others. They were not the most schooled or gifted but, much like Ron at the prison, they exhibited the love of the Lord Jesus Christ, offering acceptance, forgiveness and a caring attitude. It is this type of love that makes the Lord real to those who do not know Him or are just new in the Kingdom. The preciousness of these volunteers gave me a sense of worth and value. So often they helped me in my trials and, to this day, continue to minister and show the love of the Lord to new brothers and sisters. *May God pour out His blessings on them for their selfless and loving ministry.*

On February 4th, I was moved to the work release facility in my hometown. As soon as I walked in the door, I realized I had been transferred to another institution. Many who come to work release think they are out of prison. Actually, work release is an extension of the correction system. It is the last leg of the journey to freedom. Here you are examined under a microscope as you adapt gradually back into society. There are frequent breathalyzer and urine tests to ensure that no drugs or alcohol are being used. For me, there was no doubt. My deliverance was permanent and, though I was tested often, I never had cause to worry. It was not offensive to me to be continually tested—I felt that every time I was found to be clean, it brought glory to the Lord. The test results served to validate my declarations of a new life.

My assigned counselor was an extremely fair and honest man who was aware of my crimes and of my desire to be re-united with my family. He set down many restrictions but all in the name of protecting my children. I can never fault him or the state for that. My heart's desire was to protect my own children, so I could not be upset at others who had the same purpose. Together we formulated a new parole plan and sent it to the State Capitol. They said I would probably not spend more than six months at the work release facility; this was fourteen months past my release date. *But*, I thought, *even though the state has control over my body, my spirit has a life sentence in Jesus.* The tabernacle belongs to the Lord.

While I had been at the work camp I sent out some resumes, and, the day after I arrived at the work release facility, I had an interview for an accounting job in the city. I was so excited, believing the Lord was going to immediately open the door for me to work, make good money, and not have to travel far. Praising God for opening the door, I set off the next morning for the interview.

The first obstacle I encountered was the application. I say "obstacle" because on the bottom of the sheet was the question, "Have you ever been arrested for a felony?" *What should I say? Should I lie now that I was in the Lord and healed? No, I had to tell the truth.* Next was a typing test and, since I scored in the nineties, I knew I was equal to or above the other applicants. After a brief interview the supervisor told me that, after reviewing all of the applicants, the top two would be chosen. I thanked the interviewer and left for the work release facility. Somehow, I had the feeling or, perhaps, a premonition, that I was not going to get this job. When I called them a few days later, I was told that I was among the top applicants but that they had gone with another person. I wondered, *Is it my prison record or the reason for my prison stay?* Probably both. Because I was at the work release facility, I had to let each prospective employer know that I was in prison and to expect a visit from the correction officer to ensure that I was actually working for the firm.

I had gone to the interview with a patched-together outfit since all of the clothes I owned were still in my wife's possession. She listened cordially when I called her. "I need you to bring my clothes and some shoes. I've been going on interviews, and tennis shoes don't make too great of an impression."

"I understand. I'll be there this evening."

"Could you bring our daughter? It's been a long time since I've seen her." I hesitated. "Also, I think we need to do some talking about our relationship—or whatever is left of it. I have to make some plans and go on with my life."

"I'll be there as soon as I can," she said.

I waited patiently until 9:00 PM and then called to see if she was still coming. Rebecca answered and told me that her mother had gone to the movies with her boyfriend. Needless to say, it was difficult to stay joyful in the Lord; however, I went to the Lord with my anger and resentment.

Forgiveness was the utmost thing in my mind. By His grace, I kept myself from sinking into bitterness and anger. So many other things that needed my attention helped me stay focused on who I am in Christ.

Over the next few weeks, in between job interviews and during the evenings, I managed to have a number of conversations with Susan. Nothing I said could convince her that I was different or that our lives together would be different. She had become settled in the life-style she was in and did not want to change, especially for one who had been so destructive to her and her children. I could not blame her although I kept praying that she would understand the truth of the deliverance of the Lord Jesus Christ and how she could profit from my marvelous transformation. I had brought her so much sorrow and now I wanted to bring her so much joy. On one occasion we had just a few minutes alone and I quietly told her how the Christ in me was now going to seek her best good and that I would be a loving servant instead of a tyrant. We looked closely into each others' eyes and, as we bent forward to kiss, I could feel that the truth of the Lord had reached her heart. However, at the last moment she pulled back and screamed "No, no, no, you just want to hurt me more! You want me to trust you again so you can get back at me, but I can't trust you. Leave me alone; get out of here!"

There was such an ache in my heart for what we had both just lost. In a way her loss was worse than mine. I had Jesus but she was alone. We never again came to an understanding of what the Lord had done for me. From that time forward we became adversaries, in the sense that those outside of the Lord and those who belong to the Lord are following conflicting paths.

Chapter 25

The Perfect Job

One of the things that had drastically changed for me was the amount of fellowship I had with other believers. Whereas at the work camp we had four meetings a week, no volunteers came into the work release facility. I still had my own routine of reading the Bible, studying correspondence courses, memorizing Scripture and praying—all of which kept me focused on the Lord. A song that I had often heard described my emotions: "If none go with me, I still will follow." This is how I felt—alone but still determined to follow my Lord. I had to wait for two weeks before I could get out to church, so I spent most of the time talking to my kids and reading the Word. It is important that those inmates who go to work release facilities hold on carefully to the relationship they have developed with Jesus Christ or they will be swept away with all the trappings of freedom. The family can be a real obstacle if they do not follow the Lord. They can influence an inmate into getting back into the same things that led to his arrest. They don't understand that Jesus has given this person a whole different direction in life. I cannot emphasize too strongly that those on work release immediately align themselves with other Christians in the facility or with believing family members.

At this point, inmates are so close to the final step of liberty from incarceration that it is tragic to lose sight of Jesus and be dragged back into the miry clay that held them for so long. In Galatians 5:1 it says, "Stand *fast in the liberty wherewith Christ has made you free and be not entangled again in the yoke of bondage."* Don't become lost on this threshold to freedom. Jesus doesn't want to lose his converts on the brink of Canaan. Let us all go on into the promised land.

During the first week, I met a girl named Esther who was waiting for her release to come from the State Capitol. She only had one or two months left before she would be free. When Esther saw me reading my Bible, she asked if I was a Christian.

I smiled. "Yes! Yes! Yes!—I really love the Lord. He has given me the strength to get through the most difficult situations."

She sighed. "Even though I'm a Christian, I've felt alone here. At the women's prison I was used to having regular studies, but I've no real fellowship here. If only someone from a church could come and take us to services."

My heart was moved for her and so I called some of the pastors I had met at the work camp who ministered in the area. They promised to come down to see her and take her to church. One week went by and no one came. Two weeks went by and still no visitors. Before the third week passed, she had gotten into a fight with one of the inmates and hit him with a bottle. Then, knowing she was in for trouble, she took off. It was heartbreaking to see her run and ruin everything so close to the end. Here she was waiting for help from the Christian community but none was forthcoming. It is deplorable that no answer came but we need to remember not to put our trust in people, no matter how holy or important they seem. This invites disaster.

The Lord loves us and does not want to see us fail. When David was hounded and chased by Saul, he encouraged himself in the Lord. Esther's inability to stand with the Lord was going to cost her much time. My prayer was that the Lord would perfect His love in her through the trials she was now facing.

By the end of the third week, I still had not found a job. Praying daily, I expected each interview to be the right job but it seemed I was either over-qualified or under-qualified. It was difficult to get a job as an executive again because most of the applications asked if I had ever been in prison. Frustrated, I kept calling out to Jesus to be my provider. The following day my counselor told me to stay in for a meeting with the team leaders of the facility. Since I had been obeying all of the rules and passing every breathalyzer and urine test, I wasn't worried. *They're probably just wanting to encourage me for trying so hard,* I thought. But it wasn't about encouragement; it was about my account balance for room and board. It was getting too high and, if I didn't have a job by two more weeks, I would have to be sent back to prison. Then, after about six months, I would get another chance since I had not been in any trouble.

Immediately I went to my room and presented myself humbly before the Lord. "Have you brought me this far only to send me back again, Lord? Have I failed You so badly at this place that I need to be back inside prison for more growth? Speak to me Father." The Lord was silent. After examining all that I had been doing—truly searching my heart—I determined that sin was not the cause. Not that I was without sin! But when I became aware of having done something wrong, I went to the Lord in repentance. The purposes of the Lord don't always line up with our way of thinking. Though He was working more trust in me, I did not know it. But I did know Him as my provider and I was sure He would not let me down at this point in my journey to freedom. I had to thank Him for this turn of events because He is always worthy of praise. Many places in the Bible tell us to thank God for and in all things. His ways are perfect, making wise this simple man. That night one of the men came in and told me he had seen a sign in a Seven-Eleven window saying, "Help Wanted." Immediately, I knew that the Lord had begun to work His miracle for me. Rushing out and full of excitement, I told myself Jesus was about to lead me over the Jordan. I went in and asked for the manager. "I've come about the job that you have advertised in the window."

"I'm sorry but we filled the job an hour ago. You can leave your application though and, if I need anyone else I'll call you." Feeling very disappointed, I slumped down and shuffled out of the store. Yet something inside of me would not give up. *God*, I thought, *I know you will not forsake me. You are my glory and the lifter of my head.* As I looked up toward the sky, I felt strengthened. Suddenly, I saw a sign across the street which read, "Help Wanted." I crossed over and talked to the manager of the fast food restaurant, telling him that I had been in prison and was now out on work release. "If you hire me," I said, "the counselor from the facility will come and inspect the job site."

Without any hesitation, he looked me squarely in the eye. "If you are willing to be an honest and hard worker, I will give you the job. Be here tomorrow about three and we'll train you for your shift."

"I'll be here," I said, thanking him over and over. As I rode the bus home, I praised the Lord for seeing me through all my trials and being my provider. Back at the facility, I told my counselor that I had gotten a job and that I would start the next day. He gave me a set of papers to fill out. I put them away and then called my brother Bob to give him the good news.

"Hey, I got a job today so they won't be sending me back to prison! Isn't God wonderful?"

"That is good news! Where will you be working?"

"At one of those taco places. I start tomorrow. They only pay about three dollars an hour but, at least, it's a job."

"How are you going to live on that?" he asked.

"It's enough to keep me out of prison while I continue looking for an accounting job."

After a long pause, he said. "Listen, I want you to come to work for me. I'll pay you five dollars an hour to start."

I was hesitant. "But I don't know anything about painting. How am I going to be of any help to you?"

"You can be a laborer for me until something better comes along."

I knew he was only doing this because he thought I was in a jam. The truth was that he couldn't afford another employee at the time. Later he told me that the Lord told him to hire me and promised that He would supply enough work. And, sure enough, as soon as I was hired, the Lord brought more than enough jobs—in fact, we even had to hire additional workers. My brother's obedience provided, not only for me, but for his family as well.

As I looked back I could see that the Lord had worked a special thanksgiving in my heart. He was teaching me to be truly thankful for his provisions. The job He gave me at the taco joint was a true blessing and, after witnessing my gratitude, He gave me an even better job. I truly believe that "*every good gift and every perfect gift is from above, and comes down from the Father of Lights, with whom is no variableness or shadow of turning.*" (James1:17)

It had been the desire of my heart to get a job working in a Christian organization. One month after beginning work for Bob, I was offered a job at a local church council. They offered me a position as a bookkeeper for $1200.00 per month. Since I was used to making over $3000.00 per month, I was taken back a little by the salary. Yet, I thought this was an answer to my prayer to serve God with my accounting skills. When I went in to apply, they told me they had dropped the salary to $1000.00 per month which I thought was unreasonable. Although it proved to be a mistake, I turned the job down. It took another nine months before I got another offer in my occupational field. And yet, God, in His infinite wisdom, used this time in my life for a higher purpose. My son was also working for my brother and we had time to get reacquainted.

This was the perfect situation for Tom because he had complete control regarding the amount of contact we had. The pace of our developing relationship was his to determine. This time became so precious to us, as we got to know one another the way we were now, not as we had been. He could see that the Lord had truly changed me and that he had no reason to fear what I might do to him. We could laugh together and play together without him feeling threatened. I praised God that he was becoming relaxed in my presence and learning to trust me again. I also thanked Him that no other employment had robbed us of this time together which he needed to confront the hurts and wounds that Tom had suffered at my hand. There were some trying times when he would pull back and make me aware that there were still areas that were going to take work. I realized that such wounds are deep and that healing takes time and patience; however, I knew that God would restore my son to wholeness—a wholeness that would allow him to preach and share the testimony of Jesus Christ without hindrance.

After about two weeks of working together, we came back to my brother's apartment complex. There was a sauna and a jacuzzi in one of the buildings and, since we were tired and hot, we went to relax together. We sat in the sauna, pouring out the water and basking in the steam. There was a gnawing need in me to tell my son just how sorry I was. I turned to him. "Tom, I only wish there were some way to completely erase the sorrow I have brought you. There is no way I can change the past, but I want so much to be a part of your life now and to ask you to forgive me for all the wrong I have done to you."

He turned to me, tears in his eyes. "That's all under the blood, Dad. I forgive you."

The tears flooded down my cheeks, tears of joy and relief. There was hope; there was a chance that we could have a normal father and son relationship.

"Thank you—thank you for your willingness to forgive," I sobbed. As time went on, I realized that my son represented the beginning of the true restoration of my children. From the oldest to the youngest, the Lord was beginning a long and loving journey for my children and myself—a journey of hope and restoration.

Rebecca and I were also getting to know each other again. Although she was understandably cautious about renewing our relationship, I prayed for God to open her heart to His love through me. It was important to allow Rebecca to make all the choices regarding our relationship.

Chapter 26

A Church Family

One of the necessary ingredients to staying in the Lord after release from prison is to be aligned with a Bible-believing church. While in prison, the body of believers are very close and supportive. It is important to have similar support on the outside because of the increase in opportunities to sin. When I first arrived at the work release facility, I had no privileges—that is, I did not have any free time. I had to wait for two weeks to get any personal time and then only with approved sponsors. Because so many have abused the excuse of going to church, the authorities are not impressed when a person pleads for time off to go to church. They will have you wait until you have earned the right to be out of the facility on the weekend.

From the beginning, my brother was anxious for me to attend church on a regular basis. He volunteered to drive the forty miles to pick me up at 8:00 AM, take me to church, and then return me at 6:00 PM. This helped to get me established in the church and taught me to enjoy the fellowship of the other brothers and sisters in the Lord. I really thank him for all that effort. Much of my success is because of him and his unselfish ministry to my family and me.

Because I didn't know anyone that first Sunday, I was not very outgoing. When some people came up and welcomed me to the congregation, I didn't know what to say. This was strange since I am rarely at a loss for words. When the service started, I stood up and announced who I was and thanked the people for praying for me during my incarceration. Assuring them that God had heard their prayers, I asked them to praise Him for delivering me out of the prison. Very slowly, I came to know this body of believers. At first I thought of all these people as being pure, holy, and righteous saints who had never done anything wrong. *Oh, how wonderful that they would accept me, this black sheep, into their assembly.* It was rather intimidating to be around these perfect people. However, as time went on, I learned that most of them had been in their own prison of sin before the Lord bailed them out. I came to the total realization that we have all come to the Lord Jesus Christ through His blood, mercy and, grace. "*All have sinned and come short of the glory of God.*" (Romans 3:23) We are the children of the Lord through Jesus.

After I had been at this church for awhile, I began to listen to the whisperings of Satan telling me that I did not belong there. He would say that they only liked me because of my brother and I started to believe him. During this time, I was invited to speak at a couple of churches to give my testimony. In fact, I missed almost a month from my church. When I finally got back, I looked around at the sincere and loving faces of the people whom I had really missed and thanked the Lord for allowing me to be back home. From that point on I became more friendly and outgoing, developing new and deeper friendships in the church.

I had established another routine of spending ten hours a day working and commuting. Finally, I went to my counselor and asked him if I could drive my brother's car back and forth to work. His reply was that I could only drive if I had my own car and paid for the insurance. The prospect seemed hopeless since I did not have this kind of money to spend. However, when I prayed in Jesus' name and sought His will in the matter, I felt that there was a release to have a vehicle. I knew that He would work out the details. Bob was all for putting some money down on a car and making payments but I did not want to be in debt. The next Sunday, one of the people from the church approached him with a question. "The Lord has been revealing to me that your brother needs a car. Is this true?"

"As a matter of fact, it is. We were hoping to find a car so he could meet me at our work sites and not have to use the bus so much."

"Well, I don't know if you would be interested, but my neighbor has a car and he only wants $200.00 for it. It's not really fancy, but I know its a good running little car."

My brother was enthused. "We'll come and look at it right after church." What we found was a 1967 Chevrolet Belair that had been parked all winter. Water had accumulated in the back seat and, needless to say, the aroma was far from pleasing. However, the Lord opened my eyes to the marvels of His gifts and I could only view it as the chariot of the Lord. It was a vehicle of ministry and purpose in which I delighted. My folks advanced me the money and I took possession of the car.

When I called to get insurance quotes, I was stunned at how much they wanted. Because I hadn't been insured for so long, my premiums would be high for awhile—too high for me to consider. Then my brother called his insurance agent who suggested that I be added on to his policy for a minimal charge. I was in business!

Driving to the jobs made things a lot easier. I got more rest and could read the Word in the privacy of my own room. Once again the Lord had provided in a most innovative way. There is just no way to limit the miracles that the Lord will do for his own. I just praise Him that His caring has continued on and on in every area of my life, not just the physical but in the spiritual as well.

The months raced on and summer was drawing near. One May evening, driving home from work, the Lord spoke to my heart. “It is time for you to be out. I am releasing you from the work release.” A peace settled over me that set me free from worrying about the paperwork in the State Capitol. My God had set me free and no one could hold me any longer. That night my counselor called me into his office and said that my papers had come from Olympia and that I would be released in three days. “I know.” I said.

“How could you know? ”he asked. “I just got the papers this afternoon.”

“Jesus told me on the way home that He had released me. I trust in His Word.” The counselor grumbled something and dismissed me.

I finished the week out and got ready for release. My folks were told to get ready for their house guest and, on May 28th, I was released and assigned to a parole office in the downtown area. Although the actual release had become anticlimactic in the light of the Lord’s revelation, I was very pleased to get out.

Chapter 27

Paroled at Last

It was time to begin the next leg of this journey with Jesus Christ. There would be fewer restrictions and more opportunities—not for sin but opportunities to demonstrate that the work of the Lord in me was real. This parole officer was going to be a challenge for me. Though she was now with the State Department of Corrections, she had come from the State Department of Social and Health Services. More specifically, she was from the State Department of Children's Services and had had to deal with many families where abuse had occurred. She was going to make sure that I did not reoffend on *her* caseload! Our first meeting was short and to the point.

With confidence I said, "Please be assured that I won't be a problem to you. Jesus Christ has made a marvelous change in my life."

She wasn't overly impressed. "I know you won't be a problem but the reason is because of the restrictions I'm going to impose on you."

The first restriction related to contact with my children and wife. I could not be a pest to them and had no authority in their lives. I could only talk to them if they wanted to talk. If my wife felt that I was being intrusive to their life-style, I would have to wait for them to call me. It was frustrating but I knew the Lord was working out a special purpose in this training.

I could easily understand the next restriction which stated that I could not initiate any physical contact with my daughters. Even my youngest daughter had to feel safe in my presence, and it was imperative for my older daughter to be the one who determined if and when there was going to be any contact with me.

I was required to continue in counseling with the Christian doctor. The state left it up to his therapeutic judgment as to how often and how long I would need to see him. At the beginning there were two visits every month with the sessions lasting two hours but, after a couple of months, the sessions were reduced to one hour. This counseling helped me in so many ways. One of the main benefits was having an outlet for the frustrations that I encountered in adjusting back into society. The added pressures of trying to reunite with my family made it all the more necessary to have someone to help me confront my feelings and to deal with my emotions as they presented themselves. Before I had always suppressed them. It was wonderful to learn that my feelings were normal, considering the situations I was going through.

Abstaining from alcohol and drugs was a requirement which posed no problem for me because of the work of the Lord. Every other week I had to report to the parole officer and inform her of any problems I was having. Fortunately, by God's grace, there were not many problems to report.

The last requirement was to take a lie detector test every ninety days to be sure that no deviant behavior had been taking place. If these restrictions weighed on me, I would remember that all authority was from the Lord and He had placed others over me. If a person claims miracles in the name of Jesus regarding behavior, the individual should not be hesitant to have that behavior monitored. The only result can be to the glory of God. This was my attitude thanks to His Spirit.

The first lie detector test came about two months after I was paroled. Even though I had done nothing wrong, I was nervous. Being hooked up to all the wires didn't help my state of mind. *What if the enemy causes me to be nervous and it seems as though I'm lying?*" I thought. However, the presence and peace of the Lord prevailed and I realized that He would not allow the marvelous work He had done to be tarnished. When I entered the room, I was only slightly nervous. The examiner explained the test and its purpose, telling me to try and relax. He asked me some sample questions so that I could get a feel for the test.

When he felt I was ready, He explained the next step. "We're going to ask you some specific questions regarding your parole restrictions. Here they are: (1) Have you used any alcohol or drugs since your release? (2) Have you molested your children? (3) Have you been having deviant sexual thoughts regarding children?" He told me to breathe normally and answer truthfully.

"Am I allowed to add some questions to the test?" I asked.

"Yes, you can add whatever you would like."

"Okay, let's add these to the list: Have you had any sexual thoughts about children since your conversion in November of 1984? Have you had any sexual fantasies of women other than your wife since your conversion in 1984? Have you threatened or physically intimidated your wife since your release?"

"It isn't necessary to be so precise. You could never pass these kinds of questions. We all have sexual thoughts about women—it's impossible not to have them."

"In the Lord Jesus Christ it is possible to have a pure thought life. His work in me has been final since the day He delivered me from my sins. I insist that you ask me these questions."

"As long as you realize that you have to bear the consequences."

One by one I answered the questions with the word "no."

One by one the lines were printed out on the tape. *No change, no change.* When he got to the questions which related to sexual fantasies of women or children since my conversion, he took a big, deep breath. Both questions were answered no and both times the needle did not move on the tape.

When the questions were finished, he removed the tape and went over the results very carefully. He turned to me and said, "I have no doubt that you haven't violated any of your parole requirements. I am also sure that you haven't been involved with impure thoughts since your conversion. I don't understand but I've been doing these tests for over twenty years and I'm certain that all of your answers are truthful. How do you explain this?"

"It's the renewing of the mind by Jesus Christ. Through His Word, our minds become changed to focus on the things of the Lord. Pure and wholesome thoughts reflect the character of Jesus Christ. As a believer, I knew and trusted that I would be completely transformed."

He looked puzzled. "I—I feel that there must be something to what you're saying. I've never seen anything like this. I will make my report to your parole officer."

Excitedly, I went to see my parole officer, so very proud of what the Lord had done in me—something that could now be measured by others as proof.

But she wasn't buying the report. "There has to be a reason why the test didn't work," she said, looking at me suspiciously.

"There is—His name is Jesus. Doesn't it mean anything that the examiner is convinced that I was being truthful?"

She dismissed my question. "I'm not sure what went wrong on this test but we'll do it again in a couple of months and see if there is any change."

Once again, I tried to explain that the change was in me; however, she wasn't interested in what I was saying. And, though my test results were always the same, the examiners kept expecting me to fail, being unable to reconcile my success with my past behavior. The name *Jesus Christ* fell on deaf ears. What I was experiencing, however, was a growing understanding in my own self that the Lord's change in me was permanent, remarkable and, most of all, final!

Shortly after being released to my parent's home, I was sitting on the back porch, reflecting on what was happening in my life. There was the limited visitation, the constant scrutiny, and the seeming hopelessness of my marriage. I felt so very lonely and unloved. Here was all this honest love being offered so freely with no takers. I knew if I could only initiate this new relationship, it would be so fulfilling for all of us. Tears began to trickle down my cheek. There was such an ache in my heart. Slowly a verse began to come to mind that I had read so often. It was Matthew 23:37, "*O Jerusalem, Jerusalem, the one who kills the prophets and stones those who are sent to her! How often I wanted to gather your children together, as a hen gathers her chicks under her wings, but you were not willing.*"

It became clear to me how much the Lord desires to give us His love but, so often, we are not willing to receive it. This wondrous Creator of all things is waiting to give us an inheritance for eternity and we are too busy or uncaring to accept His gift. The Lord understood my loneliness since He had been rejected and even despised by the very people He came to save. There is no area of my life and no emotion that the Lord Jesus Christ has not experienced. As the Psalms, the prophets, and the Gospels are read, Jesus' suffering, rejection, loneliness, and sorrow are revealed. So often people say they can only relate to others who have suffered the things that they have gone through.

There is good news for all of us. The Lord Jesus Christ has suffered every hurt and sorrow, even beyond those that we have had to endure. He knows sorrow. He knows the sting of the whip. If you will open up your heart to Him, He will come in with healing in His wings and apply His loving balm to every hurt. *Was it physical, sexual, or emotional child abuse? Was it abandonment? Was it a lack of love?* What has the Lord Jesus Christ not suffered? And He suffered these things for our sakes—not for any unrighteousness of His own but for our transgressions. He willingly and even joyfully (Heb. 12:2) took our place. Our suffering builds character; His bought redemption for us. In Hebrews 4:15-16 it says, "*.....but was in all points tempted as we are, yet without sin. Let us therefore come boldly to the throne of grace, that we may obtain mercy and find grace to help in time of need.*"

I want to implore all of you to take advantage of this compassionate cry of Jesus Christ. Oh James! Oh Susan! Oh John!, Oh, Jane! Oh, (Your name) Understand that the Lord Jesus Christ knows your hurt and wants to heal you. He knows all of the sorrow you have experienced and wants to comfort and relieve you of the pain. He speaks here both to the abuser and the abused. Usually the abuser has also been abused and is in need of healing. Let this sweet, loving, caring God enter into your life today and let the deliverance flow.

The first week that I was home on parole, God told me to go back into the work camp and share my new experiences with those who had been left behind. Specifically, one of the brothers' wives had just left him, and the Lord knew he needed encouragement. When I was still in the camp, one of the brothers who had been released came back to minister. He had greatly encouraged me and now it was my turn. I was being called to be an encourager. Prison was the last place I wanted to minister—I never wanted to see the inside of a prison again. And yet, I could not stop the urging and commanding of the Lord within me to call the prison authorities. In my state, one must be out for at least one year before he/she can be allowed back in the prison system as a volunteer. The State wants to be sure that no underhanded motives such as friendship, revenge or profit are pressing the person to get back in the prison. When I contacted the prison, they told me that I could come up the next Sunday. I was thrilled to have the chance to visit my friends and tell them how great life was on the outside when you have Jesus Christ.

I had the privilege of ministering there in the work camp for the next six months. When officials realized I had not been out long enough, they promptly said that I could not come back until I had been out for one year. I accepted that and thanked the Lord for the time He had given me to minister.

About that time, my ex-roommate, Tim, asked me if I would like to go with him into the state prison. I told him I would be delighted. I was supposed to be filling in for a few months, but it turned out to be a ministry that has continued to this day.

When I had been out a full year, I was called back to minister in the camp where I have been sharing ever since. Sometimes it is special for the inmates to hear from one of their own who has made it on the outside. I praise God that His faithfulness sustains me.

Chapter 28

Accountability and His Promise

With all of the counseling and monitoring going on, I felt very confident of God's work in me. I stayed out of difficult situations, looking for accountability first. There was no reason to put myself in an inappropriate situation. Even though I knew that the Lord had changed me, I did not want to invite temptation. However, the real proof would have to come when I had some interaction with young children. Such an occasion came several months after my parole. An old friend, Jim, who knew of my prison stay and crime, invited me to come and help him with a picnic for the children of his youth group. Most of them were between the ages of 6 and 13. Bathing the situation in prayer, I asked the Lord to reveal any weakness that might still be lingering in me. No matter what the consequences, I could not offend again. This was actually going to be my first direct confrontation with children who were the same age as my victims. My faith in the Lord's work was now going to be tested.

We arrived about 10:00 AM. It was a warm day and that meant shorts and tank tops for most of the kids, which added to my nervousness. I knew the work of the Lord was real but this seemed so confrontive. I wished I had not agreed to help. Jim and I worked together unloading the food. Then we set up the barbecues and coolers for the lunch. Most of my time was spent clinging to Jim. As the children began to arrive one by one, I prayed and asked the Lord for calmness. Fear of ungodly thoughts was uppermost in my mind. One failure, one error and I was terrified that everything would be undone. Satan was trying to throw my past at me. Since my sins involved child abuse, he decided this would be my weak area, and wanted me to believe that I still had the same unholy desires which took me to prison. But my precious Jesus wanted me to know that my desires were now after the heart of God. He revealed to me that thoughts may come and go but only by dwelling on and entertaining such thoughts do they become sin. My fears were never realized.

As the day wore on I was becoming aware of a special feeling in my heart for these children—the same wholesome and caring feeling I used to have before becoming a child abuser. My concern was for their best interests. It was all so wonderful and so special to see children as children again. I was praising the Lord under my breath as we played a fun-filled game of baseball. Jim and I were captains. We helped the smaller children so that they would feel successful in their endeavors and, overall, it was a most rewarding day. It is important to emphasize that I was with a person who knew about my past and held me accountable for my actions. He was watching and, in no way, would he have given me the opportunity to hurt any of the children. A child molester, even one totally delivered, should never allow himself or herself to be alone with young children unless someone is present to monitor the situation. This book is written, not to put children at risk, but to save them from the same pain that I inflicted on my victims.

Time has revealed how necessary it was for me to be in that situation. Seeing proof of my God's work, I could hold my head up and walk strongly. Thoughts and emotions that seem so normal to others represented a true miracle for someone who has sunk to the depths of wounding children. Just to care again, to have contact without evil intent, and to shelter and protect as God had ordained brought me immeasurable joy. So simple, yet so foreign. Now in Christ Jesus, this marvelous transformation was being fully revealed. *Thank you Jesus!* I praise you, not only for my healing, but for all who would turn their hearts to You so that they might experience this same transformation. It is possible! Through Him all things are possible. There does not have to be one more painful episode, no more shame and regret, and no horrible secrets. This living and risen Savior wants to meet you now right where you are. Take this time to acknowledge Him as your personal savior, believing that He will forgive your sins and lead you into the paths of righteousness for His own sake. He loves you and wants to stop the pain and hurt, both in you and your victims. Cry out to Jesus now and let the healing begin!

That first summer out was so exhilarating. I thanked God for having the opportunity to do many father-son things together. From time to time I would have my youngest daughter with me, although this was somewhat more difficult because of the animosity between me and her mother. I tried to keep things on a peaceful basis but there was so much hurt between us that it seemed impossible not to fight every time we got together. Of course, we were really hurting our little one because she loved both of us so very much. It is difficult for the children to be put into a position of choosing one parent or the other. Nevertheless, my own short temper contributed to much of the problem.

By this time my wife was living with a man whom she intended to marry. He wanted to be a father to my daughter which caused even more problems. One day I got a phone call from Jennie and the two of us were trying to make some plans for the next time we could be together. This was usually once about every three weeks for just a few hours. On this particular day, she seemed kind of short and was making smart-alek replies. When I tried to correct her, she became quite loud. Trying to use God's wisdom, I told her I was her father and loved her very much. Her response was devastating. "You don't even know what love is all about. My new dad is ten times the father you ever were. I don't even want to see you anymore."

She hung up the phone and I sat there speechless, feeling intense pain. Through my tears, I cried out to the Lord, begging Him to somehow help me through this hurt. I held tightly to the hem of His garment. With perseverance, I made it through and about a month later Jennie called me and apologized. Realizing that my arguing was causing her pain, I sought the Lord's help in this area. His direction was simple. *Stop arguing!* No matter what the provocation, don't argue. The next weekend, when I was scheduled for a visit, I would give it a try. However, her mother called, saying that I would have to sue her in court because she was never going to let me see my daughter again. The rage overwhelmed me. Every curse word I could remember came flooding back to my memory. But the Lord glued my mouth shut. I couldn't seem to answer for a moment and, by then, His peace and the word about not arguing took over. "If that's the way you feel, I'll wait for you to change your mind. I'm sure the Lord wants me to have time with my daughter. You have my number, call me when you want to make new arrangements." Hanging up the receiver, I went to bed with an incredible freedom in my spirit. Not bound by rage or anger, I could simply allow the Lord to handle the problems of my life. By that weekend, she called back and made arrangements for a visit. The Lord was faithful to His promises.

From this time on, Susan and I had better communications. Instead of waiting for her to change or the situation to change, the Lord changed me. Most times the Lord is not concerned so much with the situation itself but with our reaction to the situation. *Will we shine forth with the character of Jesus*

Christ?

When the Lord gave me a promise that He would give me possession of all of my children, I could hardly believe it. *With my past, how would that be possible?* In Isaiah 49:22-23, I read, "*...they shall bring your sons in their arms and your daughters shall be carried on their shoulders, Kings shall be your foster fathers and their queens your nursing mothers; They shall bow down to you with their faces to the earth and lick up the dust of your feet. Then you will know that I am the Lord. For they shall not be ashamed who wait for me.*" He had given me Scripture which promised me protection in prison. *Could I dare to believe Him for this miracle? A man convicted of child abuse able to get possession of His children? Was my God big enough to do this?* I called a friend who had been in the Lord for many years and told him what I thought the Lord had just revealed to me. This person felt that the Lord had truly made an overt promise that my children would be restored to me. I am not just talking about restoring the relationships, but restoration so that we would live together as a family. Tears of joy began to flood my eyes as I realized that this was a definite promise and, from that day on, I began to share His promise with my children. They were excited and were willing to believe with me that the Lord would put our family back together.

However, I took His Word and began to run with it, thinking I was completely in His will. To end the problems with visits, Susan and I had decided to divorce. In our state, only divorce decrees can address visitation. Without this court order, the parents must work things out for themselves. Since we were not doing that, we had to use the court system to regulate the visitation. However, I took it upon myself to petition for custody of my daughter and to provide reasonable visitation for my wife. The court was stunned. My wife's attorney immediately brought out my past conviction for child abuse. And then my attorney brought out the treatment I was undergoing. Back and forth it went until the judge asked to have an independent psychiatrist examine me. His recommendation was unfavorable and was forwarded to the family court representative who examines all of the information for the court and then makes a recommendation to the judge. Needless to say, what they recommend usually becomes the judge's decision. During his investigation he interviewed my brother and sister-in-law who told me the family court was going to recommend that I not see Jennie anymore. Unless Susan and I could come to an agreement, I would lose all contact with my daughter. *Lord,* I thought, *did I misunderstand your word? Did You not say that You would deliver my children home?* The Lord gently let me see that my own pride and obstinate behavior had brought this problem to pass. My unwillingness to cooperate with my wife in light of her concerns for her daughter's safety had brought about this impass.

Putting myself at Susan's mercy, I went to her and asked for help so that I could continue with at least some type of visitation. I could see no other way to handle it. Humbling myself before the Lord for my sin and blindness, also humbling myself before my wife to whom I also owed an apology, I explained the whole situation and asked what she thought would be fair. Instead of the sarcasm which I expected, she was most understanding and recommended very reasonable alternatives. It really came down to the fact that Susan resented me trying to dictate all the rules and schedules. I had been given another lesson in regard to putting my own agenda ahead of God's.

We went into Family Court the next day and told them that we had come to terms on visitation and would not be needing their services. Reluctantly they withdrew and we settled the matter before the judge. I ended up with better times and days than I planned on before. Understandably, my wife was more accommodating when she had some say in the life of her own daughter. The Lord's promises are sure and settled, but we must wait for His timing and direction and not run off by ourselves. He can accomplish His will in such marvelous ways and doesn't need my help or yours to bring it about.

The course of the divorce involved selling our home. I hoped to use my part of the money for the down payment on another home for the children and me. One of the outcomes of my obstinate behavior was that I used my lawyer repeatedly to get court orders and hearings to justify my position. These never accomplished what I wanted and only served to help my attorney plan a wonderful summer in Europe. In the course of a year, I had spent three fourths of my money and was no closer to bringing Jennie home than at the very beginning. The Lord had taught me a difficult lesson in regard to trusting Him and His ability to perform His own Word. In my ignorance, I had spent a bountiful provision that His graciousness had provided and the immediate hope of a new home was gone. By His grace, I hope to be more discerning in the future.

Visitation became more frequent and longer in duration, while my wife and I had fewer and fewer arguments. Because we recognized our mutual authority in raising our daughter, over the next few years we were able to focus more on what our daughter needed than on our own selfish desires of revenge or self-righteousness. An exception came when Susan agreed to allow our daughter to come with our church to our family camp. We were going to be gone for five days and it took a lot of convincing, not only from me, but church members as well. We finally came to an agreement and left on a Tuesday. It was a very special five days for me, my daughter and son. We fellowshiped, swam, fished and tanned. It was a great and relaxing time for all of us and I thanked God for our time together.

I had no way of knowing that, in this time of peace, the enemy was plotting my overthrow. Somehow Susan had come to believe that she had not granted me permission to take our daughter and had called my parole officer and the State Patrol to inform them that I had kidnapped Jennie. For four days they had been scouring the state looking for us. My parole officer was set to violate me whenever I was arrested.

When we returned, I was told to call my parole officer and to explain my activities. The matter was quickly resolved since at least ten witnesses had heard my wife give her permission. Praise God that this incident was the exception, and, in general, our dealing with visitation became very amicable. Although the enemy meant her accusation for my destruction and possible return to prison, once the matter was clarified, it served to discredit the testimony of my wife. There were other instances when she called my parole officer and reported my behavior as violent or threatening. The parole office began to take her accusations with a grain of salt, and my calm reaction to the situations began to give her confidence in the confession of faith I had made to her.

Chapter 29

The Invisible Line

The first year had gone by with the Lord giving me great success in staying away from sin and addiction. Though the enemy would have had me fall, His right hand held me up. Drinking had not again snared me into its pit of darkness. It was more than abstinence—it was deliverance. I had no desire to drink. Drugs were also foreign to me. *How could any of these things help in the process of my maturing in Jesus Christ?* I had to be free to serve and worship Him. The Lord allowed me to help a couple of brothers who stumbled when they got out of prison.

One of my best friends had been suffering from back spasms and neck strains. To help him, the doctors had prescribed pain medication for relief. For ex-addicts this is a sure snare. It is so easy to slip back into the craving for drugs when legal prescriptions are given to a person by a reputable physician. When his pain medication ran out, he thought he would try alcohol just once to see if it would deaden the pain. When he found that it worked, he tried it again. It was not long before the sorrows began to come. First there was an incident where he scared his nieces in a drunken stupor. Screaming and yelling, and pounding on their door, the poor children were huddling inside when their mother came home and stopped him from going any further.

Another week went by and I received a phone call. This man's mother was on the phone, sounding very upset. "I hope you can help him," she said. "His sister just called to tell me that he's stuck in the road by your house. Please help him." Going right over, I found him in the street, his car blocking both lanes. The rain was coming down and he had a flat tire, apparently running off the road and swerving back on. He barely recognized me as he stood there trying to figure out how to work the car jack.

"Let me help you," I said. "Sit behind the wheel till I tell you to move."

He lumbered to the driver's door and sat down. After changing the wheel, I took him to my house, gave him some coffee and tried to make him lay down to sleep. When he refused, we almost ended up in a fight. Defiantly, he threw open the door and raced to his car, not realizing I had his keys. Finally, I sat next to him in the car and began to pray. Placing my hands on him, I rebuked the spirit of alcoholism and commanded it to leave. He seemed to brighten up just enough for us to communicate. Since he still refused to stay with me, I woke my son up to help me with the drive to the next town. We delivered him to his folks who were anxiously waiting for his safe arrival. *How many times had this scene been played for them before he came to the Lord.* Now, in Jesus, this same misery was being poured out again on his parents. Was there a difference? They didn't know but they soon found out. He went to his college minister and admitted the problems he had been having and left himself open for various sanctions. Because of his honesty, they gave him no punishment. They encouraged him to call on them before he started to have problems, not in the aftermath.

This brother, and others who had stumbled, sent very sobering messages to me. It broke my heart to see them failing.

It made me realize that, whether in the Lord or not, when a person is full of drugs or alcohol, he is subject to the spirits that control him/her. If I wanted to be successful, I would need all of my faculties to hear the Word of the Lord through His Word and Spirit. The only recourse I had was to develop a program that would put some things beyond an invisible line that was out of my reach. Drugs and alcohol were the first things my mind sent beyond the line where I couldn't reach them. This simple tool helped me to avoid certain downfalls.

There was one area that I had not delivered over this line nor submitted to my Lord. The area I am referring to is relationships. I began to feel that, though the Lord had asked me to wait for my wife to change, this was not going to happen. In my mind, this made me available to be with someone else. I met a Christian woman who was very new in the Lord. She had come out of some very difficult situations and found me to be refreshing and desirable. Her attention began to blind me to the Lord's calling to holiness. Having been focused on keeping out of sin from the prior pervasions, I had not prepared myself for the battle of sexuality between adults. It was only a short time before we became sexually involved. I was devastated and could hardly face my God. *How could this have happened. Was all the love I felt for Jesus a lie*. I was so confused. The enemy was right there to condemn and assure me that the Lord was now aware that I was a phony and that I could never go to Him again. That night I was very close to walking away from my faith, but my hunger for forgiveness took me back to the foot of the cross. I awoke to such shame. The filth was suffocating. "Oh Jesus, oh Jesus, forgive me," I cried.

After a couple of days, I began to feel as though the Lord had heard my cries. Because God promises in His Word that He will never forsake me, I picked up the pieces to begin again. After going to the woman and apologizing for misleading her in Jesus. I thought I had dealt with the problem. In the past, using and manipulating a woman in a weak position was my speciality—my trademark. But that was before Jesus!

We thought that holding hands, kissing, and embracing would be all right as long as we did not let it go too far. Without Godly standards, these self-limitations did not work and we sinned again. In fact, we quickly got into a cycle of sin. Sin, repent, and sin again. Seven times we fell and I found it difficult to talk with God. *Could I ask for forgiveness when I just kept on sinning?* Repentance is turning away from sin, not looking for a cover-up. This time I went away and sought the Lord, experiencing true repentance, and receiving forgiveness. As so often is the case, He forgave me sooner than I forgave myself. Our church had communion soon after this and I could not bring myself to partake. In I Cor. 11 it says, ". . . *he that eateth and drinketh unworthily is guilty of the body and blood of the Lord.*" Because I felt unworthy, I refused to defile my relationship with the Father.

In my heart I purposed to follow through on my repentance —not a few days but permanently. I called the woman up and told her I would not, could not, continue any physical contact since we were not controlling the extent of that contact. She responded that, if I wouldn't touch her, she did not want to see me again. It was the end of our friendship. Many times I agonized over the hurt I caused this woman, acknowledging that I had muddied the name of the Lord. As a Christian man, I should have reflected Christ but, in reality, I had used her just like all the unsaved men had used her in the past. Now she would question what real difference there is between the clean and unclean.

About six months later I met another new Christian woman and we began seeing each other. This relationship headed in the same direction; however, by His grace, we did not commit the same sin. This time, although taking a stand for God, I failed in the relationship. *Why was I failing?*

One day my son Tom came home with a paper from school. It was a letter from a young man who had asked how far was too far. The author listed his personal standards and told the young man to set his own personal limits in the light of the Word of God. I couldn't believe what I read. Limits. Of course. The thing that was missing in all of this was limits. Unsaved, I felt no need for limits. But now I had to seek His face and have Him help me with setting limits. He made it easy. Abstinence. No touching, no kissing, no hugging. Love with a pure motive.

As I was trying to assimilate this into my walk, my brother Bob comfronted me. "I see the problems you've had with the women you have met. Surely, you realize that, until your wife divorces you, being with another woman is adultery."

I had no answer. Inwardly, the Lord witnessed that Bob was right. *How much better would things have gone if I had honored my marriage vows?* It didn't matter what my wife was doing; I was a Christian and I had His Word. Realizing that I had failed, I withdrew from relationships altogether, waiting for my wife to become saved. The wounds that had been inflicted both before and after my prison separation made it impossible for her to come back to me. A divorce petition was filed and we began to await the outcome.

Chapter 30

Definitive Proof

It was the end of my first year of active parole; I was still seeing my Christian counselor twice a month. The State, before taking me off active parole, wanted to be sure that I had truly progressed and was no longer a threat to society. Although my doctor gave a good report and recommended that I be released from parole, the parole officer wasn't sure if that was enough. She wanted to have some identifiable evidence that I was all right.

At this time a new test called penal plethysmograph for sexual deviancy was brought into popular use. Basically it is a lie detector hooked up to the genitals that is used to measure arousal with various kinds of stimulation. The stimulation is in the form of pornography. My immediate reaction to such a test was negative. Since I had been delivered from pornography, no way did I want to pollute my mind or become entangled with it again.

My counselor advised that this test was considered the definitive proof whether or not a person is truly in recovery from sexual addiction. He explained the procedure and said the decision was totally mine. "You've already proven that you are all right," he said. "But if you passed this particular test, it would silence all your critics who say there is no recovery from deviancy, only abstinence."

This was a crucial matter and required much prayer. I wanted to know the Lord's desire and, through His word, was given direction. He gave me Ephesians 5:13 which says that "... *whatsoever makes manifest is light.*" And so, somewhat nervously, I decided to allow myself to be subjected to this test. *What if this proved I was still a pervert? What if I have only been fooling myself and all the wicked thoughts are really hidden in my mind?* I looked to Jesus to help me be calm. When I entered the testing room, the man doing the testing put me at ease with his calm attitude. Somehow he gave the situation dignity, giving me a complete explanation of what would take place. Overall, I felt God's assurance, but there was still some natural apprehension.

The test took about two hours. During that time, I was shown pornographic images of subjects close in age to my victims. This was followed by older models in sexually explicit poses and finally finished off with both violent and homosexual episodes. During the test, you must discuss your feelings, and answer questions regarding what you see and what you feel. When it was over, the test-giver asked me to wait while he interpreted the results. Upon returning, he told me that he appreciated the fact that I did not hide behind my faith. Then he spoke the incredible words. "Your reactions to the material, in relationship to children, had a rating below that of how *normal* adults would respond." I could only praise my God. This was also another assurance to me that His work was real and complete. The enemy cannot accuse me any more in this area. The other reactions were also within normal ranges and his feeling was that I had somehow developed a system that kept me from entering into thoughts and reactions that could lead to reoffending.

When I left the office, I read his evaluation which included a brief history of my offenses. It had been so long since I read these things, and the words caught me off guard. I began to weep. I wept for my stepson and stepdaughter who had been so badly wounded. I wept for the children in the pictures I had just seen—victims of a perverse society. This horror of pornography has so gripped our country that the most deviant and perverted desire is filled in abundance by the purveyors of pornography. This country must repent of this sin and oust the magazines and movies that defile the minds of our men and women, especially the youths. They are misled to believe that physical love is real when, in reality, it is only of value in the marriage relationship. This truth must be told.

My counselor was ecstatic with the test results. "This is even better than I had hoped for. I knew you had grown and made a real decision for the things of the Lord. I realized that the Lord had done something wonderful in restoring you, but now the test results will make others aware of the truth of your healing."

Though I tried to join in his enthusiasm, I could not get past the faces of my children and the realization of how much I had hurt them. And then there were all those images that had been shown to me. I prayed fervently that the Lord would erase them from my mind. By His grace, it seemed as if I had never seen anything. Because of the pornography, this is not a test I would recommend to others. It was necessary for me to take it, but others must do as they feel the Lord leads.

When the results were sent to the parole officer and the courts, they told me that the test wasn't very accurate. They were looking for some way to discredit me and tried to dismiss the test; however, my God had His plan working all of the time. The man who administered my test was the number one technician in the state. My parole officer had also worked with him when she was in Child Protective Services and knew that his skill and integrity were above reproach. No one could now refute his results. With this in mind, I was granted release to the inactive status. Here I would stay one year with no reporting. If, after this time, I was still doing well, I would then be totally released and all of my rights restored. With this last success given to me by Jesus, I was ready for the challenge of being accountable when there was no one to be accountable to.

In Christ Jesus, the molester, the drunkard, and the drug addict was put to death. In Romans 6 the Lord tells us "*. . . that our old man is crucified with him that the body of sin might be destroyed that henceforth we should not serve sin.*" (Romans 6:6) For every man and woman out there, know for sure that through Jesus Christ, not only will your sins be forgiven, but your whole life will be changed. Jesus Christ will not just cover the sin in you but He will destroy it. In Him, and through His power, you can be set on a new path and never will you have to look back. We are truly "*. . . crucified with Christ nevertheless we live, yet not I but Christ lives in me. And the life I now live in the flesh I live by the faithfulness of the Son of God who loved me and gave himself for me.*" (Gal. 2:20) We must get a firm grasp of this concept. Not by our strength or willpower but by the faithfulness of the Lord Jesus Christ we will triumph. Satan can have no hold over the possessions of the Lord. "*Sin shall not have dominion over you. . .*" (Romans.6:14)

I don't care what the bondage or what hold the enemy has had in your life; if you want freedom, there is Jesus. If you want hope, there is Jesus. If you want a fulfilled life, there is Jesus. Everything that you need, want, or hope for can only be found in Christ Jesus. Do not set yourself up for a fall by constantly looking over your shoulder for the sins of your past to overtake you. When the Lord says to "*Set your affections on things above and not on things of the earth . . .,*" (Col 3:2) the idea is to have your eyes fixed on Jesus.

Chapter 31

Communication

Therapy with my counselor continued from June through December. There were many different programs at the clinic and I decided to take one of them which dealt with the different options we have when we minister. It also touched on parenting and the means of evaluating how we are doing with the decisions that affect our work, both in and out of the Lord. I thoroughly enjoyed these classes and made many notes to help me with the parenting of both my stepson and daughter. My progress was so evident that they offered me training in their methods with the purpose of becoming part of the staff of the clinic. I was very honored and was ready to leap at the opportunity; however, the Lord put a check in my spirit and I said I would let them know.

When I took the time to seek the Lord, I felt Him saying that this was not His direction for me. Regretfully, I declined the clinic and waited to hear from the Lord. He knew my heart was to share the help and source of my progress. It was not a long wait. There was opportunity after opportunity in the prisons to talk to the men one on one. This was a whole new ministry for me. Then I got a call from the coordinator at my old work camp who asked if I would take over the Sunday service for one of the ministers who was going away. I was not sure about this. To share a little here and there or to talk one-to-one was easy for me, but to stand up and give the Sunday sermon was quite another matter. I'm sure my reply was less than enthusiastic. "I have never done that before. I'm not sure I can."

"Listen, if we didn't think you were capable, we wouldn't have asked you."

I deferred to their judgment and agreed to take the service. This struck me as a commendation from the Lord. With three weeks to prepare the message, I began with prayer and more prayer. Then, after unsuccessfully reading the Word to see if some scripture or passage would jump out at me, I finally just sat down and began to write. As the futile attempts began to mount on the floor, I got up and went for a walk. *What is the message supposed to be? Where does the Lord want to take the body in His word?* Finally, the idea began to formulate in my mind. Ezekiel, Jeremiah, Job, Jacob, and on and on. All these men obeyed the will of the Lord at a great price. Their obedience was necessary in order for the Lord to accomplish His purposes. Because of the impending divorce of one of the men, the part where Ezekiel loses his wife and is not allowed to cry or mourn for her became a central part of the message. In all I spent about four hours working on the actual sermon. There was a feeling of confidence that what the Lord wanted to communicate, He had gotten into my spirit.

Praying all the way up to the prison, I asked for His anointing to communicate His Word and not my own. Upon arrival, I had the church service announced and went to the schoolroom where we met. It was ten minutes before the first man arrived. A few minutes later another brother came in and we began. We had some song books and tried our best to praise the Lord without accompaniment. Our hearts were in the right place even if our voices were nowhere on the scale. With some trepidation I took my place at the podium. It's funny how dry the throat becomes when you stand in front of others. The sermon lasted forty-five minutes, which is about twenty minutes longer than one of the men. He had something else to do, I guess. Thinking that the other brother would soon be gone and leave me to an empty room, I began to perspire. Fortunately for me he stayed until the end. We prayed together and closed with an embrace. So many thoughts were swimming through my head. *How could it have gone so badly?* I was so busy trying to analyze the failure that I hardly noticed the brother talking to me. "I can't tell you how delivering that Word was. I have been in mourning ever since my wife left me two years ago. This Word has set me free to release that hurt and continue on with the Lord. Thank you for sharing His Word."

I could hardly believe my ears. It seems that the Lord can use even the most nervous vessels to get out His Word. It also became apparent that one does not need to have a large audience to communicate His Word or to bring deliverance in His name. The Lord will save us one by one if He has to. Our success is not measured in numbers but in the obedience to His Word. From that first humble beginning, other invitations followed until I was offered one Sunday a month to preach. I gladly took the challenge and tried to share from a practical point of view on how to walk in the Lord after being in prison.

During this time, Tom had been living with Bob, while he and I worked together and became reacquainted. My heart ached for God's promise to be fulfilled so that Tom would be with me. A division between my son and brother soon escalated to the point that it drove my stepson to move in with me —a new and important step for us. Even though it had been four years since the abuse had stopped, and even though my son was in the Lord and had accepted his healing, the reality of living side by side was a test. We did well most of the time. I tried my best to be the kind of father I had read about in the

Bible, encouraging my son in the Lord and trying to live the life I preached about. He was marvelous in obedience to authority, even when he felt I might be mistaken. *What a precious young man he had become*.

As a little boy he had been different than his playmates,. sensitive and caring about their feelings. I wanted him to be rough and aggressive. When you grow up in the projects, that's how life is. Failing to let him be who the Lord had made him, I tried to put him in my mold. Now I could see that the sensitivity I had disliked was a gift that the Lord used to enable him to reach others. His empathy for their hurts, heightened by his own hurts, continually allowed the Lord to use him in ministering to hurting teens who came into our church.

Life was good for both of us. Then one night it was 2:00 AM and he hadn't called or left a message on the phone. At 3:00 AM, when he finally came home, I was relieved but upset. "What happened son? Are you all right?"

"I just had to do some thinking Dad. I couldn't come home."

"What's the trouble? Whatever it is I think we can work it out together."

"Dad, I was afraid to come home. I thought you were going to hurt me again."

At first I could not answer him. Then I realized that it was just a lie of the enemy. We spoke about that and how the Lord would not have allowed us back together if there were danger involved. He calmed down and we both went to bed. After that, we worked together in prayer with our pastor and others in the church for his complete healing from the old wounds. In the Lord's graciousness, the time has come when those scars are just opportunities that allow him to minister to others.

Please be aware of the process here. Even in the Lord and with the family all around my stepson, the healing took time. I know the Lord can miraculously heal in an instant; however, in this case, the Lord slowly worked His mercy in my son. He provided an opportunity to prove that I loved him in the hard times. In light of the length of time and depth of scars in my stepson, I cry out to anyone who might be abusing children to please get help! Turn yourself in and bring hope and the beginning of recovery to your victims If you are being abused, tell someone. No one has the right to hurt or violate you. The Lord wants the hurting to stop. Speak out for your own freedom.

Chapter 32

A Vision Realized and a Vision Lost

Keeping busy in the church and in ministry helped my walk with Jesus. Unstructured time provides opportunities for temptation and so I continued to press on in Jesus Christ. The renewal that had come from His Word was being worked out in my daily walk. I took part in the music ministry at church by running the overhead projector for Sunday services. God also had given me the opportunity to go to one of the other prisons three and four times a month. Many of the men found my testimony a source of hope for themselves. As I shared my testimony and the successes and failures in the outside world, the inmates were given a ray of hope that penetrated the prison walls. I tried to let them know that if they will hold onto Jesus, no matter what problems appear, they will not be defeated. In Christ we have the victory, regardless of the outward appearance of the situation

About this time, I joined a group of volunteers at the work camp who had begun to raise funds for a chapel. There were six of us in all. We had two to do the administration and four of us to actually go out into the community and ask for donations. I worked with the group that went to the churches to declare our need for both financial and prayer support. As we spent hour after hour on the phone contacting different churches, we found that not everyone was as interested as we were to see this house of God be built. In fact, only one church in ten allowed us to come into their congregation. However, the Lord allowed us to understand that not every house was called for this project. The Lord had just the right people at just the right time for us. Time after time we would run out of money only to get a call from some congregation that was now ready for us to come and share. It took about three months on the average from first contact to presentation. Some churches gave us free will offerings and some sent us to their mission boards. Regardless of the method, we were always provided with the funds or material we needed.

On one occasion we were allowed to speak at a Bible study before the main service. As we prayed before the meeting, the Lord revealed that this would be a different offering—not one for money but for building materials. We shared for about an hour and, sure enough, they did not take up an offering. Afterwards, we stayed and answered questions. One of the men came up to me and asked what materials were going to be needed next. I replied, "They told me that we need sixty sheets of 5/8 inch sheetrock."

He then handed me his card. "When you are all ready for the sheetrock, call me and I will give you all sixty sheets." Then, after thanking us for our presentation, he walked away. We didn't know how to thank him. As it turned out, he not only sent up the sheetrock, but all the material for mudding and taping. In this way the Lord helped us build His house.

The work of the inmates was instrumental in the building of the chapel. Volunteers selflessly helped from the beginning to the end, saving on costs. In fact, the chapel is a tribute to God through their labor. The original idea came from one of the inmates who had a vision for the building and pressed the administration until it became a reality. He had since left the camp but returned to attend the special dedication. The fund-raising took us to about sixty churches. It was such a joy to stand up and give my testimony and relate it to the building up of the body of Jesus Christ through this chapel. We tried to communicate our vision for this building as a house of ministry where lives would be touched for years to come. Included in our group was a wonderful couple who did some of the speaking and all of the music for the presentations. The man had written some songs that so perfectly captured the heart of the prisoner in Christ. Almost every time he finished, I would have to wipe the tears away from my eyes. In fact, it was so moving that it was hard for me not to financially contribute each time.

The beginning of the year brought about the closing arguments of my divorce. Though I had continually tried to make my wife see that, through Jesus Christ, a new creature had been created, she was unable to find enough trust to believe that truth. I remember one night when I had taken Jennie home, Susan and I went to the store together so she would not have to carry the groceries two blocks to their apartment. Her boyfriend was gone for the evening and she needed the help. As we loaded the trunk with the groceries, I turned to her and said, "So many hurts have occurred on both sides but Jesus is able to heal all of them. I want you to know that, in Jesus, I forgive you for any and all hurts that I perceive you have given me. Let's go back to your apartment and pack up your belongings. You can move home with us tonight."

There was a look of unbelief in her eyes as she realized that I was sincere. "How can you say that? How can you want me? So much has gone on between us."

"It is the Lord. His desire is for our marriage to work—for this family to be one in Him. I know it seems like an impossible situation, but if we just do what is right in His eyes, He will work out the details."

As she stared at me, for just a moment there was a glimmer of hope, a flicker of belief. Then, just as quickly, it was gone. She shook her head. "It could never work. You would just be the same old person. We could not get along." In February, the divorce was final.

At this time, Rebecca left her mother's home. They had an argument over Rebecca's boyfriend, the end result being that Rebecca left and stayed out of touch. It was not until two years later that we heard from her again. At that time, she and I began to rebuild our father-daughter relationship. It was slow but steady progress toward reconciliation; however, before we could firmly bond again, Rebecca moved with her fiance to the midwest. We have had only limited contact over the last few years.

I have come to realize that the abuse Rebecca suffered has made it difficult for her to choose healthy relationships. My heart's desire is for Rebecca to receive God's healing for those wounds I caused her. As you read this, I hope your heart has been touched and that you will lift her name before Jesus.

Chapter 33

Merry-Go-Round of Bureaucracy

Although I had reasonable visitation rights with my daughter, the court did not allow for overnight visits. As the year went on, however, Susan allowed her to have overnight visits on a regular basis. In fact, I was taking her for the whole weekend twice a month. Jennie was becoming a part of the church youth group on the weekends she was with me. My concern was for her to be in a home that put Jesus Christ first. My ex-wife, though professing to be a Christian, did not exhibit the fruit of which the Lord speaks.

As the summer turned to fall, there began to be a struggle between my daughter and her mother. Jennie was not respecting her mother's authority and was also having trouble in school. It seemed that she had been telling lies about her homework for three weeks. When the school finally called to let Susan know that they were concerned with Jennie's failure to turn in her homework, we sat our daughter down and discussed the matter with her. Explaining that we were disappointed at her behavior, we tried to get to the root of the problem. Apparently our separation caused her to see herself as part of the reason for the divorce. We began to assure her that it was our own failings that caused the divorce and that it had nothing to do with her. This seemed to solve the immediate problem, but we realized the necessity of periodically reassuring her that she was not responsible for the divorce.

This proved to be only the beginning of the problems between Jennie and her mother. There was an ever-increasing distance between them. Susan was having trouble disciplining her and was continually losing control of her temper. It was beginning to worry me and I suspected that she might be physically abusing our daughter. Corporal punishment is needed at times but hitting with objects or in a rage is not proper. On two occasions, when I picked up Jennie, she had bruises, one on her arm and one on her leg. Another time she had a bruise above her eye. I was sure that she was being hit but I failed to investigate the incidents. When I asked her about the bruises, she always had an explanation. The eye bruise was from hitting the monkey bars at school and the one on her arm was from wrestling with her stepfather's brother. Even though she had a reason for every occasion, I couldn't shake the feeling that something wrong was going on. Without her cooperation, I could prove nothing.

In September I went on a short hike with a church singles' group. It was a beautiful day for climbing and we had a great time. When I got home, there were a number of messages on the answering machine. My daughter was in the hospital and I was told to get in touch with the facility as soon as possible. My call was transferred to the office of Social Services. The voice sounded concerned. "Your daughter has suffered a severe eye laceration. She told us that her mother hit her. The State has taken over at this point and she cannot be released back to her mother. We would like you to come down and see her."

A piercing pain struck my heart. My little girl was hurt. *How did this happen?* "I'll be right down to take her home," I said.

"No, you can't take her—not with your past history. The State has taken custody but we thought you could come and comfort her before they take her to a receiving home."

"I can comfort her but not take her home. That's ridiculous! She's my daughter and my past is just that—the past. I'm a different person."

"Our hands are tied. We cannot make that decision. If you insist on pressing your rights, we will have your daughter removed before you get here."

I have to calm down, I thought. *My God is always in control even if I cannot fathom His methods.* I rushed to the hospital and into the area where they had Jennie. When I saw her, I gasped. Her eye was swollen and full of blood. My heart was torn as her wounds became my wounds. I swept her up into my arms and she cried, "Oh, Daddy, Daddy. I waited so long for you. Please take me home!"

"Honey, I can't do that. They have to make sure that you are going to be all right."

"But, Daddy, I want to be with you tonight!"

"Sweetheart, I have to do what the police tell us to do. It's the way things are for now. I will talk to them and try to get you home right away."

"No Daddy, don't leave me! Please, take me home." Her tears, mixed in with my own, were soaking my shirt. I knew this wasn't the best thing for her; however, I also knew that if I did anything contrary to the police or State requirements, that I'd lose my daughter forever.

The terrible pain that I felt at the sight of my abused daughter is the same searing pain parents feel when they see their abused children. I had been guilty of hurting children and through them, their parents. Aware of the depth of hurt I had caused my ex-wife when she found out how I had abused her children, I wondered if she had done this for revenge. *Was she hurting my daughter to get even with me for hurting her children.* Yes, I had come face to face with the crushing pain that abuse causes to both parent and child—a pain too devastating to communicate or explain to anyone. Please, if you are abusing or being abused, do whatever is necessary to bring it to an end. Speak out, get help, find deliverance, provide a safer environment. Our God hates this sin.

For a brief moment, as I held my daughter, she felt safe again. The police came in and said they had to take her. She clung to me, crying for me to protect her, but as they forcefully took her from my arms, all I could do was say, "Honey, please don't worry. God will watch over you and be your protector until I get you home."

As they took her down the hall, I heard her fearfully say, "Daddy, please don't let them take me." Then, as they continued down the hallway, I heard her fading little voice cry out, "Don't leave me Daddy! Never have I experienced such emotional loss.

With my daughter torn from my arms and me helpless to do anything, I just stared down the empty hallway. Never had the word sorrow had such meaning. With all the turmoil, I had almost forgotten that my son and his girlfriend were there. We turned to each other and my son gave me a hug. It helped. The social worker came over and spoke with me. "That was the bravest thing I have ever seen. For you not to make a scene must have been so difficult. You did the perfect thing for your daughter. Any emotional display would have made this trauma even worse. You have such concern for your daughter, even over your own obvious needs. Sir, I commend you for your behavior."

Feeling numb, I mumbled something about the power of Jesus Christ. This woman knew I had been in prison for child abuse and she was still talking about my concern for children. It truly was a miracle.

My son and his girlfriend stopped for something to eat so I went on home by myself. It was difficult to drive in the dark with all my mixed-up feelings. Somehow, somewhere, from the depth of my spirit there began a word of praise for my God. *Thanking Him in every situation?* I don't know where it had come from but the words were passing my lips. "Jesus, I have no understanding how losing my daughter like this is Your will, but I do know that You have all the universe at your fingertips. I praise You for what I will learn in this of your faithfulness."

That Saturday night a spirit of heaviness descended on me, nearly suffocating me. Later, I acknowledged that it would certainly have been wise to call some brothers and sisters for intercessory prayer. Our family needed help!

Even though I felt numb the next morning, I went to church early to take part in the prayer before the service. Because I was so choked up, I prayed in the Spirit. For forty minutes I just wept and poured my heart out before the Lord. During the song service, I managed to be lifted in the spirit by the presence of the Lord. Only a few people knew about the situation. One or two came over and consoled me. The service passed in a blur and I went home where I spent the rest of the day in prayer.

Although against the rules, the receiving home did allow Jennie to call me. I know this was the favor of the Lord. On Monday, we had about fifteen minutes together on the phone. Obviously calmer, she thanked me for taking some of her personal belongs to the Child Service Office.

"Daddy, I don't like this place. When are you going to come and get me and take me home?"

"Honey, the authorities say you can't come with me right away, but you can probably stay with your Uncle Bob until we get things worked out. It will still be a couple of days until they have the court hearing. You have to stay there until then. Believe me, I'm doing all I can right now. The rest is up to Jesus Christ."

But she was persistent. "Daddy, help me please. I'm dying here." I did my best to calm her down before I hung up.

That night the Lord showed me that, indeed, He had all things in control. I could not see the whole plan but I had enough faith to at least take the next step. Submitting papers to the proper authority was the Godly thing to do, even if it didn't seem possible to achieve the desired results.

The next day Jennie called me at work, nearly hysterical. It was difficult to make out what she was saying above the wailing and tears that pierced my soul. I felt as though I were bleeding from her wounds. *Oh, my God, help us,* I screamed in my mind. "Listen, it's too hard to hear you cry like this. Tell me what street you are near and I will come and get you. We'll go to my apartment. Of course, in about an hour the police will come and I will be taken back to prison, but at least we'll have a few hours together."

All of a sudden the screaming stopped and I heard her take a big gulp. "Would they really take you back to prison?" she asked.

"For interfering in a court case like this, I would be gone in a minute and with no questions asked," I said.

"In that case, Daddy, I guess I can wait. Do you promise that they will take me over to Uncle Bob's place tomorrow?"

"Honey, I just don't know. I thought you would have gone today. Whatever time it takes, it will be in Jesus' perfect timing. Can you trust in Jesus to deliver you at the right time?"

"Yes, Daddy, I know He will."

On the way home that night, I became the child that was screaming. "Father, don't you hear the cry of my daughter? Are you blind to her tears? Why have you allowed this? Say something! Tell me what to do! Faaaatherrrrr!" Once again there were tears streaming down my face and I felt utterly trapped in the bureaucratic web of child custody. In II Cor. 1:9 Paul says, *"We had the sentence of death within ourselves that we should not trust in ourselves but in God who raises the dead."* This referred to me—I was in that place—trusting only God because I had no power. My Lord wanted to make me realize that the restoration of my family, the building of my house could only be accomplished if I leaned on His strength. Trying to get this revelation into my heart and spirit wasn't easy. I went to bed feeling defeated and wrung out.

The next morning I awoke with a new sense of gratitude for the Lord. By His graciousness, I was alive for one more day to fight for my children. Somehow, during the night, the Lord had gotten through to me. As long as I had my life, I could not be defeated by the enemy. His power is my strength. No weapon formed against me will prosper. My trust grew immeasurably that day. *The substance of things hoped for, the evidence of things not seen* had become more of a reality to me. (Heb 11:1) I began to see that in Jesus there is no defeat but that there are challenges, adventures, and opportunities for God to glorify Himself in every circumstance. The burden lifted from me and I knew that my daughter would soon be home.

Chapter 34

A Promise Fulfilled

Off I went to work and then to the court room. During the hearing, a decision was reached: my daughter should reside with my brother until they had determined if I would be an acceptable parent for her. What a wonderful victory! There would be many hearings over the next few months, but they could wait. This day we rejoiced in this particular victory of the Lord.

It was two hours before Jennie was released to her Uncle Bob to be taken home. Since I had gone back to work, I didn't see her until I rushed home after work, blinded by tears of joy. The thirty-five mile commute had seemed to take forever. When I entered the house, we rushed into each others arms, peals of laughter mixed with a flood of tears. My baby in my arms, my precious daughter pulled from the fiery furnace. *Oh, taste and see that the Lord is gracious.* The hardest part was saying goodnight, but I left, acknowledging our marvelous victory in Jesus.

It must be remembered that Children's Services were taking temporary measures to see if this man who was convicted for child abuse would now be suitable as a parent for a child who was the same age as his primary victim. The fact that they were even considering it was a miracle in itself. It pales to the final outcome, but at this point it was wonderful. The initial arrangement was for me to have visiting rights similar to what I was experiencing with my ex-wife. However, the overnight visits were suspended temporarily. I also was allowed to have four hours on the weekends with supervision.

Another hearing was held about two weeks later. This was called an agreed dependency, meaning all parties agreed that some review was necessary before the state stepped out of the picture. Children's Services was beginning to back up on their first assessment. They wanted to further restrict the visitations. I wanted the normal visitations that had already been established in the divorce agreement to include extended hours and overnight privileges. At the hearing we all presented our sides. They had evidence of my background and past, and presented their concerns for my daughter. We produced my test results, counseling information and, most importantly, the six months of overnight visits that had taken place with no problems. My attorney thought I should stay with what they offered but I told her I expected, in Jesus, that all of my rights would be restored. She was hesitant but I was insistent that she ask for overnight visits and eight hour weekend visits. When all was said and done, the judge reinstated all of my visiting rights. Representatives of Children's Services were stunned, my attorney was amazed, and I was shaking my head knowingly. *Jesus Christ is Lord of all.*

I went to work after the hearing, already making plans for that weekend. About an hour later, I received a phone call from the Children's Services case worker. "Our interpretation of the judge's ruling is that we have the right to determine when and how you will have visitation."

Words could not express the rage I felt at that moment. "Are you out of your mind?" I screamed. "We just had the judge tell us—and you—that all of my original visitation rights were restored. I fully intend to carry out his decision, starting with overnight visits this weekend."

"We have to warn you that if you violate this court decision, we will remove all of your parental rights and find the child a dependent of the State."

"How can I violate a decision that told me all of my rights are reinstated?" I asked incredulously.

"We interpret the decision to mean that we have the right to screen your visiting regimen."

I could see I was on a verbal merry-go-round. It was no use continuing this argument.

Quickly, I called my attorney who was as shocked as I was. She told me to hold on and that she would call and set everything straight. "I will let them know they can't get away with this. I'll call you right back."

Calming myself, I waited for the return call. About a half an hour later the attorney called again. "Children's Services will not change their position. I will have to call the court and have a review hearing scheduled. However, it may take two or three weeks before we see the judge. In the meantime, we will have to do what Children's Services says."

Disappointed, I nodded in agreement and waited on the Lord. I knew He would vindicate His own victory so my daughter and I patiently prayed for it to be set forth permanently. The few weeks seemed short because I was so confident in the Lord. The morning of the review I prayed with some of the church members and, even though the hearing was scheduled for 9:00 AM, I was the first to arrive at the courtroom. Praying in tongues, I went to every seat, laid hands on them, and then prayed over the area where my attorney would be seated as well as the Children's Services area. Although I looked at the judge's chair, I did not feel right crossing the short wall that separated the courtroom. Nonetheless, stretching out my hand, I laid open the heavens in the Spirit, calling for deliverance. *Surely,* I thought, *the judge will put these people in their place. How can they expect the judge to countermand his own decision?* My attorney already had assured me that it would be impossible for the judge to disallow his own decision.

One by one all of the players entered the courtroom. There was a brief introduction before both sides stated their points of view regarding the prior decision. The judge seemed to ponder things for a moment and then said, "I think that, at this time, it would be best for the court to defer to Children's Services. I order them to conduct such arrangements as they deem necessary to complete the reintegration of this family, believing they have the child's best interests in mind and will best be suited to direct things from this point on." With a swift blow of the gavel, my hope disappeared like smoke into thin air. Here I was, after all these years and dollars, back at the mercy of Children's Services. Setting my eyes on the situation, I almost admitted defeat. My attorney was at a loss to give me an explanation of this new verdict. Though she was surprised and apologetic, it did not help ease my pain. How quickly we get out of focus. The lesson I learned about thanking and praising God in all situations temporarily left me. Shaking my head, I numbly listened to my attorney plot and scheme.

Suddenly, I came to my senses. *Father, You alone have the authority. All the power of the world rests in your hands.* Walking down the eight flights, I began to thank my Father for His perfect will in my life. How sweet it was that His purposes, so much better than my own feeble plans, were at work in my behalf. He truly would build my house His own way.

The praise worked in my behalf. I found the Children's Services people to be most accommodating. When I put it into the perspective that they were looking to protect the child whom I loved, it was difficult to be at odds with them. I had to get outside of myself to appreciate their point of view. My attorney, the case worker, and I sat down to iron out the details of my gaining custody of my daughter. After they had gone over my counseling reports and test results, they were at least assured that I had taken the necessary steps to deal with my deviancy. All along, Children's Services had insisted that keeping my daughter in the family was their priority.

There was a new wrinkle brought in at this time. Our caseworker transferred to another office and we were reassigned. *Here we go again,* I thought. The new person was gruff and not very cooperative on our first meeting. He walked in with all kinds of demands and I felt the necessity to hold my ground. I spoke with confidence. "My past and my treatment have been raked over again and again. We have made much progress and I am not going back to the beginning again." The case worker, after reviewing the files, agreed.

One area that concerned her was in regard to my daughter Jennie getting counseling for the assault she had gone through. We found a mutually-agreed-upon service and the counseling began. The counselor was very skeptical of Children's Services intent to place a young female adolescent with a convicted child abuser. She did, however, agree to provide the services requested. We worked together for six months and eventually got to a point of mutual understanding if not mutual respect. She was actually very helpful in getting Jennie to deal with the hurt she had sustained, and providing me with insights and tools to enable me to deal with this child once I had her home. The whole episode was winding down and Children's Services requested the final evaluation from the counselor. She told us frankly that her recommendation was that my daughter be placed somewhere else but, in light of the request of the State, she agreed that we had worked together very well. She made mention of my sincerity and my loving and caring attitude toward my daughter and her feelings toward me. However unusual she felt this arrangement, she did agree it was time for the State to make permanent arrangement in this matter. Again, regardless of the reports and recommendations, I leaned on and trusted in my Father to deliver His own Word.

On February 23, my precious daughter was sent home with

me. Unspeakable joy filled my heart. My God had kept His promise in His perfect timing. It was like a family reunion since my son was already home. Tom was very happy and Jennie was beside herself. We went out to celebrate with mighty prayers and offerings of thanksgiving coming from all of us.

I want to stop here and glory in my God. *How could it be possible for a convicted child molester to win custody of a child? Is not the Lord the worker of miracles?* The real miracle here is a changed life—a new person both morally and spiritually. These challenges in court had been met with confidence, not in myself but in what God had done in me. Jesus is able and willing to convert each of us into His image. I will only glory in my own infirmities to highlight the power of the Lord Jesus Christ. If I can prove nothing else, Jesus in me is the hope of glory. This victory was His and not mine. He loves those who love Him and will show Himself strong in behalf of the righteous. *How can I call myself righteous?* His blood has cleansed me. His spirit continually convicts me of sin and error. His loving arms never cease to hold me. His tender care is never far from me. I challenge everyone who reads this book not to let this grace go unused. Jesus Christ has the ability to give you the desires of your heart. He wants to give you purpose and a future. Won't you call on Him today and begin the most fabulous adventure of your life?

There was one final hurdle to overcome, even after my daughter moved home. In our state, there is a division between Family Court and Superior Court. Now that I had the actual physical custody of my daughter, I needed to get the legal custody from the State. The original divorce decree had to be changed so that the custodial parent was myself. My ex-wife was willing to agree to all the normal stipulations; however, $2500.00 was required for the decree to be finalized. This helped me to realize how very valuable my daughter was to me. *Is there anything, even in the Lord, that does not increase in value when it costs us something?*

One of the dreams Jennie and I both had was for her to be a part of the A.C.E school that our church ran. She often had spent time with many of the students and thought it would be wonderful to be a part of the activities that they were involved in. This meant league sports, as well as state and national conventions for academic and sport events. Most prominent for me was the Godly education she would get from the dedicated teachers. It was such a comfort to know they would never strike or walk out on their students. This was not a job to them but a mission field. Since I had gotten to know them during the three years Tom had been in the school, I was excited for Jennie. She would realize much growth in Jesus Christ through these ministers. Now that she was home, the time came for us to enroll her in the school. It was a great day for all of us.

Each year the school has a spiritual emphasis week. They go to a camp, leaving the classroom and studies behind and concentrating on getting closer to Jesus. At first Jennie would come back with a whole new attitude which would fade by the end of the first day. Now it is lasting and making changes in her character. I must thank the Lord for the wonderful opportunity He has presented Jennie by opening the door and providing the funding for this type of education. The Bible tells us that if we train up our children right, when they are old, they will not depart from it (Proverbs 22:6). This school is assisting me in raising my child. In such a complex world, it is very helpful to have other Godly sources to influence my daughter.

Chapter 35

The Marriage

I have already discussed some of the struggles I faced in dealing with my sexuality. Constant prayer kept me away from temptation and dwelling in an area that was not appropriate for me at the time. Though I did not think it possible, the Lord put me in a place where sexuality and the need for physical contact was unnecessary. *Do you understand what I am saying?* The Lord Jesus Christ, in answer to my prayer, came in and set aside my sexual desires. I told Him that, since He is Lord of all of my life, He must be Lord of my sexual desires as well. It is not that my sexual desires disappeared, but they never seemed to come to mind. In some way, when I was willing to submit in this area, Jesus gave me such special grace. Sexual desires and fulfillment are part of the Lord's plan for our lives. Some do set it aside for the kingdom, but, in the normal flow of life, Jesus grants this for our benefit and pleasure. I have come to realize that true sexual fulfillment is found only in marriage and under His covering.

The "only one" partner in the marriage so beautifully reflects our single devotion to the Lord Jesus Christ. We can have no other Gods but Jesus; He is so jealous of our love for Him. Although the world makes intimacy look cheap and easy, its beauty, as He has created, is so very special. The special sharing is made to look as if it is all-consuming and important. The giving of life through Jesus Christ and His gospel is what is really important. In reality, only the service of the Lord is necessary.

As humans, we are so driven by the physical needs of the body that we call everything necessary. In II Corinthians 10:5 it says, "*Casting down own imaginations and every high thing that exalts itself against the knowledge of God. And bringing into captivity every thought to the obedience of Christ.*" This is where the Lord brought me. When I am tempted or my eyes stray, this verse comes to my mind, helping me bring my every thought into captivity to Christ. In the book of Job, Chapter 27:1 it says, "*I have made a covenant with my eyes, why then should I think upon a maid.*" This is referring to the looking at women in a sexual manner, the proverbial eyeing up and down. Since this was an area that had caused my downfall in the past, I had to keep in mind that the women in my church were my sisters. The enemy will tempt us at every turn.

One of the ministers at the work camp had related how he had a job in a store one summer. As the days got warmer and warmer, the women coming into the store seemed to be wearing less and less. He admitted to struggling with looking at them sexually, recognizing that it was sin, and battling with it. One day a woman came in dressed very scantily. The battle was great and he knew his only hope was in Jesus. Falling to his knees at the checkout counter, he asked the Lord, out loud, to first forgive him for his wrongdoing and then to assist him in overcoming the temptation to look at these women. That lesson has stuck with me over the years. It was as simple as closing my eyes and seeing the Lord Jesus Christ. When I look into His holiness, when I gaze into His loveliness, I cannot be tempted by the licentiousness of the world. Rather than blindly telling myself that I cannot sin in this area, I rely on the strength of the Lord Jesus Christ to help me continually overcome both the attack from the enemy and the weakness of my own flesh.

Whenever we become overconfident in our own ability to fight temptation, we are set up for the biggest fall of all. It is only in His strength that we are able to overcome temptation. In fact, in Christ Jesus, there comes a change in our very makeup, so that ungodly desires become less and less. The very thoughts of uncleanness that had been a battle for me became unrecognizable. My perception changed and I began seeing more through His eyes and not my own. In this way I became willing to set no evil thing before my eyes. Hard core pornography is not what I mean but rather the magazines at the store, the sexy billboards, and the television programming. All their images and concepts are anti-Christ. We must be willing to forego them as well. It comes back "to bringing every thought to the obedience of Christ."

As the time passed and my family was living with me, I began to think about the possibility of having a wife again. What I had to do was put that part of my life before the Lord and make sure I was willing to do whatever He wanted me to do. *How could I best serve the Lord?* Only He knew for sure. With prison ministry filling two to three nights a week and the school activities of the children, I found myself beginning to wear out. I needed ministering to—something for my own replenishing. The Sunday service was great, but I was involved there, too.

One evening, after a school function, I stopped at one of the teacher's homes to pick up Jennie. Some of the other parents had left their children there as well. A few of the parents stayed for coffee and fellowship. During the conversation, one of the ladies mentioned to me that the singles' group at her church was very focused on the Lord and that dating was frowned upon. She thought that would appeal to me because I seemed to be very serious about Jesus.

The following Friday evening, I was thinking about going to this group, though, admittedly, I had reservations about starting something new with people I didn't know. Just about the time that I should have left, I received a call from a family in our church. They were inviting me out to dinner. I hesitated for a moment before I declined. "Thanks, but I have already made some other plans," I said. Actually, my discomfort of the new situation made my plans unsure at best. As I sat there in the room, the Holy Spirit was prompting me very strongly to go to the meeting. With some reservations, I left for the meeting. When I got there, one of the men greeted me and gave me a sticker for a name tag. When I saw the woman who had recommended the group to me, I nodded, "hello."

Most of the first hour was taken up with praise and worship. It was so sweet and I could feel the presence of the Lord. It was as if I were a child in a crib and this wonderful looming presence of my Father was leaning over the railing telling me of His love. My heart was melting as the Lord confirmed His love to me. This was one of the most personal times for me and my Savior. Seldom have I felt so special to Him. I knew then why the Spirit had been prompting me to go. In fact, as the evening went on, many others got up to reveal that the Lord had visited them in a similar manner.

Needless to say, such open love from the Lord prompted me to become a regular at this group. The other men and women seemed to have a deep and abiding love for the Lord. The leaders were looking for the growth and success of the members, and the worship leaders constantly brought us deep into the throne room of the Lord. I found this place to be the *"times of refreshing in the presence of the Lord."* (Acts 3:19)

Week after week, it seemed that the Lord met with me personally. I tried to make some new friends but no friendships really developed. Being from different churches may have been the reason since we had no other times to meet but at this group. Actually, the lady who had told me about the group became sort of a friend. Since our daughters knew each other and she lived by the church, she agreed to let my daughter stay at her house each week until the meeting was over. This gave us an opportunity to share about what Jesus meant to us. With no need to play dating games, we could just be honest. We came to admire each other after awhile but neither of us was interested in becoming involved. In fact, it was refreshing to have a friend of the opposite sex where romance was not going to spoil the relationship. Dating was something we never discussed, not between ourselves or with others. She had been single for ten years and had found that Jesus Christ, as He promises in Isaiah 54, was her husband. I had also come to seek the Lord first and my interest in relationships had waned.

About six months later, the singles' group was planning a retreat. The cost was $40.00 and I did not think I could afford it; however, when the Lord made sure I had the money, I made my reservation. I even volunteered to ride over on the bus so I could fellowship more and perhaps become better acquainted with some of the other members. Desiring to step closer to Jesus, I was determined to be available—to be used by Him. It was a time for me to put aside some of my own desires and begin to seriously look for opportunities to serve Jesus. It seemed as though for a very long time I had just been giving Him lip service.

In preparation for the weekend, I fasted and prayed for a couple of days. Whenever these opportunities present themselves, I try to be ready to receive from the Lord. He has so much to give us and often times we are not ready to receive from Him. My heart had to be prepared.

The trip was uneventful. Only about eight of us went on the bus and most everyone stayed to themselves. Trying to be friendly but not obnoxious, I still couldn't get anyone interested in talking with me. I put my ear phones on, listened to some music, and watched the lovely scenery that we passed. When we arrived at the camp it had already gotten dark and everyone was busy trying to set up tents and get situated. By 10:00 PM we were all settled, so we fellowshiped for about an hour and went to bed. Even though I felt somewhat on the outside, I knew that the Lord wanted to do something with me that weekend.

The morning broke very clear. We were in a campground by a river at the foot of the mountains. It was beautiful. I got up about 5:30 AM and went down to the river. Standing at the water's edge, I began crying out to Jesus. "Lord, I want to experience your power in my life. I want to be a vessel that responds to your call. When you have a word for someone, use me. When it is time to minister love, encouragement, or hope, give me the discernment as to what is needed and how best to give this in Your name."

For two hours I was engrossed in one of the loveliest meetings with Jesus. My heart sang and my spirit soared. I felt His touch and knew His love for me. Returning to camp about 7:30 AM, I got ready for breakfast which was at 8:00 AM. The first meeting was at 9:00 AM.

I thought, *Hurry up and let's get this breakfast over with so we can get on with the things of the Lord!"* The speaker for the weekend shared on how the furniture of the tabernacle was a picture of our walk in Jesus with each item bringing us a little closer to a personal confrontation with God. *Oh, it sounded like just what I was looking for.* He ministered until lunch with the Lord working in many of us. We were being challenged and pressed to follow hard into the Holy of Holies to meet face to face with the Lamb.

Lunch followed and then some free time. I grabbed a basketball and shot baskets for awhile. After a short time, most of the group passed by, heading into the nearby town which was a tourist haven. I decided to join them for the afternoon. Donna, the lady whom I knew, had to wait for a moment so I waited for her. We then took off, trying to catch up with the the group, but never did. As we walked along the river and into the town, the Lord began giving me word after word for her. I could not contain myself. "The Lord has given me a word for you," I said. "Come closer to me, my daughter. Take another step closer to me. I have a perfect love for you. I have been waiting for you to be a partaker of the table I have set for you. Do not hold back nor fear but press boldly into my presence. I want you nearer to me, my daughter, so you may drink of the fullness of the love I have for you." Over and over the Lord gave me similar words for her and I spoke them out.

Finally she turned to me and said, "Enough! I don't want to hear anymore." She later confided that the unfamiliar experience of hearing such personal words from a man had made her uncomfortable.

We spent the afternoon together looking in the various shops, buying presents for our daughters but keeping our distance from each other. We were together without being together. Uneasy by having a man hang around with her, she would often go to the other side of the shops as if something of great interest had pulled her there. She just wanted to put some space between us. During this time I was beginning to appreciate her as more than just a friend. I wasn't ready to say anything but I was seeing her as more than just a sister in Jesus.

The whole afternoon went by and we never found any of our group. On our way back to the camp I was musing about how enjoyable it had been to spend the afternoon with this precious sister. Unfortunately, my mouth got going faster than my mind and I said, "I am glad that we didn't find the others so I could have you all to myself." It was one of those times when you ask yourself who said that stupid thing only to find out it was you. The conversation for the rest of the walk centered on less personal matters.

When we got back to the camp, we parted our ways. Dinner came and went and the evening service began. The speaker finished his teaching on the articles of the tabernacle and allowed the Holy Spirit to minister. Many of us were receiving direct touches from the Lord. I was sitting next to another sister and the Lord told me to give her a hug and say "You are precious in my sight and I love you daughter." I froze.

"Lord, this is a singles' group. She will surely think it's a come on."

Then the Lord said, *"Are you going to edit what I give you to share? Did you not ask me to use you with words of knowledge and encouragement? It's time for you to obey."*

"Yes, Lord." I turned and did as he requested. I waited for some great reaction which would assure me that this was exactly the word she was waiting for but there was only silence. By faith, I had to rest in the fact that I had done as the Lord told me. The prayer line went on until late. Going to the back of the building, I began talking with Donna again and the Lord gave me another word for her. Almost through clenched teeth I spoke, "My daughter, do you feel lovable? Can you accept that I am bringing love into your life? Are you ready to be loved?" She was speechless and I mumbled something and walked away. We talked a bit later around the campfire but this word was not discussed. The following morning we had a time of rebaptism and rededication to the Lord. We took stones and left them in a pile as a witness and a testimony of the things the Lord had done for us that weekend. The afternoon wore on and we broke camp.

The following Friday at the group meeting, I saw Donna again. The meeting seemed somewhat livelier than it had been before the retreat. God was not done with us yet. Within a few weeks, I was aware that some feelings for this women were beginning to stir in me—feelings that were romantic and not platonic. This made me nervous and cautious since I had failed in prior relationships. Placing these desires and feelings before the Lord, I withdrew from any contact with her. "Oh, Lord, you know my failings and the weakness of my flesh. I have strayed often in the past, depending on my own feelings and not waiting for a sure sign from You. Whether I marry again or not is in your hands. How can you best use me?"

Determined not to say or do anything else that would encourage this lady, I felt that, if this were someone the Lord wanted me to be with, He would reveal it in her heart until she would be moved to say something to me. About one month after the camp, we took a stroll near her home. We sat on a bench and watched the sunset. I felt like she cared for me but I was determined to wait on the Lord to prompt her to speak. There was tension and nervousness between us. I turned to her asking, "Donna, how do you feel about me?"

She measured my eyes and said, "I have come to care about you, though I am not sure what direction it will go. I want to be sure that I don't end up with a counterfeit instead of the real thing that the Lord has for me."

I agreed that caution and discernment were necessary. "And how do you feel? "she asked.

"I have begun to think about you as much more than just a sister in the Lord. I think you are very special," I replied.

That simple conversation was the confirmation I was looking for. Within a short time we grew confident that the Lord wanted us to be together. I was still nervous though since I had not yet told her why I had been in prison. When I drove her home from the group one night, I stopped her before she could get out of the car. "I'm beginning to care for you so much. We cannot go one more day without me telling you that I was in prison for molesting my stepchildren."

The explosion and tirade I expected didn't come. "I already know," she said. "A long time ago someone who knew you told me about your past."

"And you still spent time with me and let me near your home and family? I can't believe it."

She said, "I believe that Jesus Christ can radically change people from the worst to the best. And the Holy Spirit has witnessed to my spirit that you are not the same man you once were."

I was very relieved. *Could it be that I had met someone who does not trust in people but in the power of the Lord?* When so much is at stake, it is necessary to proceed cautiously. We were not only going to affect ourselves but our daughters and our families. Unknown to me, the Lord had told her to go to my pastor and find out from him what my walk was like away from the singles' group. After speaking with him, she was convinced I was a genuine Christian man. The Lord began to give her the gift of faith that the sins of my past were never going to be repeated. With a twelve-year-old daughter, confirmation had to come from the Lord if she were to enter into the relationship.

That next morning I took my daughter to school and the pastor called me aside into the kitchen. "What are your intentions with Donna?" he asked.

I drew a blank. "Well, I care for her but I don't know where this will lead. I would like to think that she cares a lot about me but I'm not sure what to do." He looked at me and said that she had come in to see him, inquiring what kind of a man I really was in Jesus. Walking away, I had a feeling in my heart that Jesus had just given me a wife. From that time forward, I had the freedom to dream about the miracle of having a Godly, precious, Christian wife to share my Christian walk. This man who had sunk so low and been brought so high by Jesus was now going to have a wife to stand with in this journey to Jesus. *How humble and special I felt!* Could one whose actions were so reprehensible actually be found lovable by someone as wonderful as Donna? My God had made me desirable to someone with taste and discernment. It was too good to be true.

Soon we began talking about marriage. As of yet we had not had a date alone. We were always with the group or with our children. Things seemed to be moving along quite smoothly. Then the accuser of the brethren reared his ugly head. Some of Donna's Christian friends, who had known me before I was saved, were beginning to warn her about me. They told her what a reprobate I had been and, while it was nice that I had come to Jesus, I would never really change from the corrupt man I had been.

During a telephone conversation, she expressed her concerns. "I am so confused," she said.

"Listen, this is just a whispering campaign from Satan. You know the Lord Jesus Christ and are not ignorant of His Spirit. You spend this night in prayer and ask God who I am and what I am supposed to be to you. I will do the same. I care about you, Donna, but I want you to be totally positive that this is from the Lord. I will talk to you tomorrow."

As I lay down to sleep I cried out to Jesus. "Lord, you know that I have let my emotions cloud my decision-making in the past. There is too much at stake here for me to be wrong. I have caused a world of hurt but have repented. I can do no more. Tell me what Donna is supposed to be to me. Lord, I do not mean to be presumptuous but I need to hear you clearly and audibly. I can't trust a feeling like 'this is right' or some friend to confirm what you have to say. Lord, please, I cannot move forward here until I hear from you. I mean actually hear from you. Speak to me Jesus."

I ceased my petition and the Lord said audibly, "She is to be your wife."

There was no more to be said. It was fixed in my heart that Donna was to be my wife. It is amazing how sweet sleep is when we can rest in the promises of God. The next day I spoke with Donna and asked her what the Lord had said to her. She said, "You tell me what God said to you."

I cleared my throat, "God told me that your are to be my wife."

She smiled. "When I was at my church last night, the Lord told me that you are to be my husband."

We did not know where to go from there at the moment. I

called my pastor and told him that Donna and I were going to be married. There was only silence on the other end of the phone. "Isn't this a little sudden?" he asked.

"We both know that the Lord has called us into this marriage. We have both prayed diligently and have our answer from Him," I said.

"Very well, if you are sure. However, we have a six-week course about marriage that we would like you to take. We have some lecture tapes and some personal times that the three of us can spend together. Are you willing to take that time and get to know each other better?"

"Of course we are. Since he was my authority in the Lord, I had no recourse but to do this Godly step before we proceeded.

The class was very informative and it helped us make some real decisions about the type of Christian marriage we desired. We were shown examples of loving and caring relationships of couples who would pray for each other, who would talk things out, and who would be committed. In fact, that was the whole premise. This relationship in marriage would only work if both of us were totally committed. The same type of commitment for Jesus had to be in a marriage relationship.

Five months after the camp meeting, we became husband and wife. Our children thought it seemed too fast, but for us it seemed a long time, since we actually had grown to know each other very well over the months of group meetings. Only the grace of Jesus Christ could have brought this miracle to pass. In a few short years, I had gone from a totally desolate man to a person with incredible joy in my heart. This was not only because of my new wife and family, but because of the confirmation and revelation of His love for me.

Chapter 36

By His Grace

I have attempted to share the miraculous changes that are possible through Jesus Christ. He is the only hope for those in addiction, for those trapped in abusive behavior, and for those who suffer at the hands of abusers. My life was restored to sanity through Jesus. Most of my family members have also been restored to wholeness by that same grace. Again, I must reiterate that I claim only deliverance from my sins and bondage. I do not claim amnesty from my abusive behavior. I admit full responsibility for my actions. All the damage to my ex-wife and children was caused by my behavior. I was guilty and have borne the punishment prescribed by our government. The release comes in the fact that Jesus died for my sins and also for the hurt and sorrow that my children suffered. His grace is sufficient to cleanse me, as well as it is sufficient to heal those I have hurt.

Yet, as always, healing only comes if we are willing to accept the cure. If the balm of healing is offered but not accepted, the wounds and sorrow will continue. At present, that is the case with my stepdaughter and ex-wife. This is not a criticism but a statement of reality. The hurt that abuse causes so often cuts people off from the very source of help they need.

From the depths of my heart, I want to plead again with

every person who is reading this book and is an abuser. Regardless of the consequences, stop your abusing and get help. Your fear is so minor compared to the ocean of pain you are causing. These children—your victims—will be scarred for years. The fear and sorrow and mistrust will bring insecurity, unfulfillment, and emptiness. There is help in Jesus Christ and in Him alone.

Many methods of treatment for sexual offenders deal only with the symptoms. The root of the problem is a sinful nature and Jesus is the only answer for this. If you will only drop to you knees right now and cry out with all of your heart to the Lord Jesus Christ, He will come into your heart and set you free from this destructive life-style. Your victims will also be set free. Even though the road to recovery seems long, it is a journey of hope when Jesus Christ is involved. The hope is there for you and also for those you have hurt. Don't let one more selfish act occur. Don't inflict one more wound. Go to someone now and ask for help. Do not condemn one more child to a life of worthlessness and emptiness. Begin to work toward building life and hope and wholeness in yourself and those around you. In Romans10: 9-10 it says, "*If you will confess with your mouth and believe in your heart that God has raised Jesus from the dead you will be saved. For with the heart man believes to righteousness and with the tongue confession is made unto salvation.*"

Today, I still continue to sorrow for those I have hurt and weep for wounds untreated. My hope is simply that the complete redirection of my life from sexual abuser to loving and caring father will give hope to all who are, or have been, abusers. They too can be made whole again. My hope is also that those who have been abused can read about the success of my stepson and daughter and know that in Jesus Christ they can be made whole again. There is truly an enemy—the devil—who wants to continue to hold people in bondage to abuse so that, not only are they separated from God, but all those whom they abuse are so wounded they will not be able to get to the cross where their deliverance awaits. For the abuser and the abused there is one hope, one path, one answer. His name is Jesus! Though negotiating through the hurts is not simple, the Lord sets the path to deliverance in simple steps.

One evening, before going to speak at one of the prisons which houses mostly sexual offenders, the Lord gave me a special message for them. He made it known to me; however, that the message was a permanent one and was to be continually conveyed to those who need to hear. The message which conveys the three steps to deliverance is as follows:

1) REVELATION: The first thing to consider is the necessity of admitting to ourselves the damage we are doing or the damage done to us. It is necessary for us to honestly confront the abuse, hurt, wound, sorrow, sin, and be willing to see it for what it is. In the case of long- term abuse, it must be seen as an extended period of wounding that was unfair and unprompted. We must be willing for Jesus Christ, through His Holy Spirit, to reveal to us the incidents that caused our hurts. This will often bring up very painful memories that may have been suppressed for years. It is time to let the light of the Lord into these hurts. Only when we frankly confront the reasons for the hurts can we deal with them. As long as we do not face them, they remain as a sore and a wound that keeps us from being whole.

2) COMMUNICATION: Once the situation that has caused the wound or wounds has been honestly faced, we can then speak to the Lord regarding how we feel/felt about the abuse or hurt. Christian or not, wounds hurt and the emotions that go with those hurts are real. There is a release in speaking out the truth of those hurts and thereby releasing them. The bondage comes from hiding them or suppressing them. When they are exposed they lose their hold.

3) ERADICATION: The last step is for the Lord Jesus Christ to erase these wounds through His marvelous healing.

This may be in an instant or through a process of time. Either way the healing will be permanent. The whole purpose of the healing is to make you whole again. You will be set free to grow and experience life in a fuller and wider spectrum. You will also be able to minister and help others who have been hurt. In Scripture, the translation most used when the Lord speaks of healing us is "to make whole." This is what His touch can do so we may indeed have life and have it more abundantly.

Above all else, get in touch with Jesus Christ. For me, no other outlet, no other source could have brought me back to sanity. I praise my Savior for His grace and mercy for me, a wretched sinner.

"*May the grace of the Lord Jesus Christ, and the Love of God, and the fellowship of the Holy Spirit be with you all.*"
(I Cor. 13:14)

Chapter 37

The False Accusations

Although I would have preferred to end the book with the previous chapter, I am forced to include an addition to this saga. Throughout the book, I tried to convey my desire to do all I could to help my children overcome the damage I had done to them. In the process of fathering and training, I made mistakes that cost us dearly.

After my daughter, Jennie, came to live with me, I found it very difficult to say no to her desires. The guilt I felt for abandoning her and the family while I was in prison kept me from denying her most anything she wanted. If I said no, she would throw a tantrum and I would end up giving in. In fact, when I met Donna, she was appalled at my daughter's behavior and my lack of parental discipline. Eventually, Jennie began to miss her mother and wanted to see her. Even though our court order required supervised visitation, I felt that, since my daughter had grown to 5'3," she would now be safe from physical abuse by her mother. Cautiously, I allowed Jennie to contact her.

At first, Susan would not respond. But, after about six months, they began seeing one another for a few hours at a time. By the time a year had gone by, they were asking for overnight visits. At first I hesitated, knowing that Susan lived in a small studio apartment with her boyfriend. After some coaxing, I agreed, hoping that the renewal of a relationship with her mother would help ease the tension between my daughter and Donna.

During the next year, Jennie began to exhibit antisocial behavior upon returning from her overnight trips. More and more the rules of our Christian school were causing her discomfort. Her rebellion at home was also beginning to increase. Though I suspected that it was a situation being fed by her mother, Jennie would not confirm my suspicion. Conversations with her mother revealed that she was encouraging the rebellion rather than trying to help our daughter work through the conflicts. The teen years are tough enough without having someone feed your anxieties and frustrations. When divorced parents engage in such manipulation, they think they are getting back at the other parent when they are, in fact, causing much damage to the child. I would urge all divorced parents to reconsider their attitudes and help one another in supporting home authority.

By 1993, my daughter's behavior was becoming a family problem. Her open animosity to my wife and me, and her refusal to accept any expression of authority from us was keeping the family in constant conflict. It was at this time that she began to request to leave our home and move in with her mother. Since her mother was involved in drinking and drugs, I could not agree to such a move. My daughter's insistence grew until she began to threaten that, if I would not allow her to do what she wanted, she would tell the police I had abused her. The situation degenerated until communication was nearly impossible from either side. Determined to stand firm for my family as a whole, I went into a twenty-one day fast, trying to break this spirit of division. Things seemed to improve, but only for a short time. Making sure that I was proceeding in the Lord, I asked for prayer from our church and family and began fasting at least one day a week, not only for this situation, but also for the other family members. It had been such a miracle of the Lord to put this family together, and I did not want to see it broken up. But, I wanted to be sure of my motives. *Was I jealous that my daughter preferred her mother's home to mine?* I had to be sure it really was in my daughter's best interest to stay with me.

Jennie's threats and attitude grew worse. One weekend I picked her up and realized that she had been drinking. She denied it but we later found wine cooler bottles in her room. I then called her mother and put some new restrictions on their visitation. That was the move that set the final challenge in motion. Her mother realized that she was in trouble and could lose some, if not all, of her visitation rights.

A few weeks later, the worship team from our church was invited to lead worship for a Holy Spirit conference in a nearby city. Because of the distance, Donna and I decided to spend the night there rather than drive the fifty-mile round trip each day. With some apprehension, we allowed Jennie to spend the night at her mother's home. The conference went great, and we were well-received by the conference groups. We were blessed by the powerful speakers. The main theme on the last day was a teaching on the enduring of difficult situations. We were not aware that the Lord was arming us with power.

After the conference, we left Tom with the members of the worship team who were staying behind for dinner on Saturday night. Enroute to our home, we stopped and called my ex-wife to see if we could pick up Jennie and save her mother the drive to our home. They told me that they were just having dinner and she would be home later. About 9:30 PM I called to see if they had left. My ex-wife then said that she was not bringing my daughter back home. When I talked to Jennie, she also told me that she hated me and our home and did not want to come back—ever. Trying to reason with her was to no avail. Due to the lateness of the hour, I decided not to make a scene that evening and waited until after church the next day to go and pick her up.

Although I waited at my ex-wife's house for a number of hours, no one showed up. *Where is my daughter*? I wondered. I returned the next evening with my court papers and a police escort. My family waited outside the apartment building while the police went to the apartment to retrieve my daughter. In fifteen minutes the police returned and said that Jennie had accused me of physically abusing her. They said that they were going to leave her in her mother's care and that they would call in Child Protective Services to investigate my daughter's claims.

With a great heaviness, I drove the van home. I was so wounded that I could hardly speak. My daughter, the precious child whom I had fought so hard for, had turned on me. Her accusations could possibly cause my arrest and return to prison. How could she be so selfish that she would jeopardize the whole family—and my personal freedom—just to get what she wanted?

As the lessons from the Holy Spirit conference came to mind, I stood on the promises of God and the assurance of His saints. We called Tom, who was still at the conference, and requested him to present our family to the assembly for prayer. We petitioned that my daughter might come to her senses and that He would heal my wounded heart. Many of the men from our church were instrumental in supporting me during this very difficult time. May the Lord bless them and their families for the support they gave us.

Two days later, Children's Services notified us that the investigation determined the charges to be unfounded and said that I should go and pick up my daughter. With great relief and praise for the Lord, we, as a family, went to pick up our daughter. She was most disagreeable and made quite a scene before the officers who told her to grow up and behave.

For the next few days, Jennie stayed by herself. Believing

that we could find a solution to her disenchantment, I spent time with her, trying to work things out. I thought we were making progress; however, after five days, I came home to a note that read, "Daddy, I love you but I can't live with you anymore. I love you, good-bye."

With tears in my eyes, I went back to the prayer line. *My precious daughter was gone again.* Although I checked with all of her friends, no one seemed to be aware of her plans. For the next two days I was frantic. *Had she run away to the street?* I used to live on the street when I did drugs and it is not a pretty place. I prayed for her safety. After two days I called her mother, only to have Jennie answer the phone. Upset, I tried to talk with her but she hung up on me. Taking my court papers, I went to her mother's apartment to pick her up. While I waited, two policemen entered the apartment to retrieve her; however, they came back and served me with a court order which claimed physical abuse. "We just went through this—the claims were determined to be unfounded," I explained.

"None of that matters. You have to honor the fourteen day order and appear in court."

I was not sure what my ex-wife and daughter were going to try at the hearing. Due to my past, it seemed wise to retain an attorney to coordinate the defense with my original custody order and the abuse order entered against my ex-wife. The present court order listed Jennie's claims of physical abuse and also made an innuendo regarding sexual abuse. This really infuriated me. It was very discouraging to have to explain my past all over again.

The two weeks passed quickly in prayer and we received many words of encouragement, prophecy, and knowledge regarding the upcoming court hearing. The Lord also spoke to us through His word in our prison ministry meeting. The Lord used Exodus 14 to remind us that He had hardened Pharaoh's heart to bring him to complete destruction. In like manner, the Lord was telling me that He hardened the hearts of my daughter and my ex-wife to destroy the enemy that was in them. From that point on I walked in a great calm. I knew that my God was about to do another miracle in my life.

The morning of the hearing, one of the teachers prayed that the truth of Jesus Christ would prevail. When we got to the hearing, I was served with another paper which now claimed sexual abuse. I was devastated. More lies, more treachery from the enemy. The Lord had to keep reminding me that it was the enemy who was against me here and not my daughter and her mother. Though they were being used as instruments of destruction, they were not the enemy. Before we went into the courtroom, the lawyer, my wife and I prayed and sought the Lord's will in this hearing. When the judge read the accusations and heard our rebuttal, he calmly said, "I will have one of my court social workers investigate these accusations. All of the parties will return to court tomorrow."

Though dismayed that we would have to wait another day, I trusted that the truth would now become known. The court social worker interviewed my daughter and her mother. She then interviewed Donna's daughter and myself. She also had some of my past reports to go over. Once home, we continued in prayer with the whole church.

Arriving at court the next day, I was greeted with a new affidavit claiming sexual abuse. I prayed that the judge would not be swayed by this cheap attempt to discredit me because of my past. We also received the report and recommendations of the court social worker. She basically stated that the abusive behavior of my past had been dealt with satisfactorily and complimented my stepdaughter for her maturity and honesty. The social worker stated in her report that, from her point of view, Jennie was a spoiled brat who wanted to get her own way and that her mother was feeding the problem. She suggested my ex-wife receive counseling for her drug and alcohol dependency.

Praising God for the insight of this court officer, I was surprised at her discernment. The prayer for truth had prevailed. The judge then asked my ex-wife why she hadn't gotten treatment since it was ordered in 1989. She responded, "They took my daughter; I didn't see the point."

The judge said, "The point is that you need help!" He followed with his decision: "I'm throwing out this protection order and remanding the child back to her father and the existing parenting order."

I was so happy to hear his words. However, as we left the courtroom, Jennie said that, if I forced her to return home with us, she would run away. My initial reaction was to grab her by the scruff of the neck and lead her home. She had caused everyone enough misery for now and it was time for her to grow up. My attorney and another case worker intervened and mediated with us for an hour. We finally decided that my daughter would stay for the next few days with some friends of the family. We would then determine what to do with her.

The Sunday before the hearing, Donna and I had gone forward for prayer. We stood next to another couple; the word spoken over them was that they had been anointed to minister to children of all ages. They were a family with four children already and the wife was pregnant with the fifth.

After Jennie had spent two days with our friends, we decided to place her into a group home for five days where we would meet with her each day for mediation. However, the brother and sister from church who had received the word about ministering to children called me to ask if Jennie could stay with them.

"Would the stress be good for your pregnancy?" I asked.

They seemed sure. "We know what we're getting into. Why don't you pray about your decision?"

After praying, I decided to give them an opportunity but the group home would be a back up. Jennie spent the week there and we talked every other day. By Friday, she agreed to be at home and to follow our rules. As of this writing she is home with us and we have kept the channels of communication open. We also have been involved in weekly joint counseling and pray for a complete healing of this situation.

This was a difficult chapter to write; however, I could not, in good conscience, leave readers with a false sense of harmony in regard to the problems we have faced. This does not take away from the miracles or the glory of God. It just reaffirms that abuse has more casualties than the direct victims.

Post Script

You, the reader, have come to the end of my testimony. The miracles of the Lord have been many and His grace has showered me from the day of my salvation until now. I can say with the utmost confidence that this same grace will lead me home to my loving Savior.

I would like to make one final plea to all who read this book. If you are an abuser, seek immediate help before you strike another wound to a child's heart. Let no excuse keep you from seeking help for this deadly and vile sin. If you know of someone who is abusing, there are no circumstances that should keep you from exposing that person. Although the breakup of the families that may occur is tragic, the continued destruction of even one child is beyond price.

If you have been a victim, cry now to the Lord Jesus. Your cry will not fall on deaf ears. Jesus weeps with you and for you and wishes to deliver you. Seek His face where deliverance, forgiveness, healing, and true love can be found.

I ask for your prayers for my family and myself. We have come so far, yet there is much left to be done. The enemy continues to attack us in many ways. Jennie and I still struggle as father and daughter. Pray for my wisdom in raising her and the ability to communicate my love to her without jeopardizing the other relationships in our family. Also, pray for my ex-wife and her daughter, Rebecca, who continue to suffer from the effects of my abusive behavior.

Finally, I say now and forever that I LOVE YOU JESUS!

APPENDIX A

I would like to share a revelation that the Lord has given me regarding the healing from abuse. It is not meant to be the complete or even the best answer; it is just my sharing what God has put in my heart for the abused person.

HEALING AND WHOLENESS FROM ABUSE

1) Revelation

A. Take responsibility for your life. Phil. 3:13
B. Achieve peace with the Father. Romans 5:1, Romans 15:13
C. Seek Him for clarifying the hurt. Mt. 7:7, Jer. 33:3,6

2) Communication

A. Face reality: Identify the source of the pain. Ps. 31:5
B. Grieve for your losses. Lam. 3:48, Ecc. 3:4, Isaiah 22:4
C. Pour out your heart to God (and others). Ps. 62:8, Ps. 102:1

3) Eradication

A. Confess your part of the problem (bitterness etc.). 1 John 1:9, James 5:16
B. Forgive the offender. Mt. 6:14-15, Mark 11:25-26
C. Put love into action. 1 John 3:18, James 2:17